DATE DUE

10/8			

Demco No. 62-0549

Protect Your Social Security, Medicare, and Pension Benefits

TOM and NANCY BIRACREE

CB

CONTEMPORARY
BOOKS

CHICAGO

Library of Congress Cataloging-in-Publication Data

Biracree, Tom, 1947–
    Protect your social security, pension, and medicare benefits /
Tom and Nancy Biracree.
        p.   cm.
    ISBN 0-8092-4037-8
    1. Social security—United States—Handbooks, manuals,
etc.   2. Medicare—Handbooks, manuals, etc.   3. Old age
pensions—United States—Handbooks, manuals,
etc.   I. Biracree, Nancy.   II. Title.
HD7125.B53   1991
344.73'0226—dc20
[347.304226]   91-8553
                                                                              CIP

Published by Contemporary Books, Inc.
180 North Michigan Avenue, Chicago, Illinois 60601
Manufactured in the United States of America
International Standard Book Number: 0-8092-4037-8

To Bill Biracree,
a great father and a good friend,
who inspired this book

Contents

─── ≡ Introduction ≡ ───

Protect Your Benefits
Before It's Too Late

Although many people think of Social Security as simply a retirement program, it is in fact an invaluable package of protection that also provides vital income for the families of workers who are disabled or who die before retirement age. Nearly everyone grumbles about the amount of Social Security taxes deducted from every paycheck, yet the average family would have to pay several hundred additional dollars every month to replace Social Security benefits with private insurance plans from private companies. In 1990, 23 million retired Americans received Social Security checks. And 15 million other Americans received monthly benefits under Social Security's disability and survivor benefit programs. Many of these recipients were children and spouses of workers who became disabled or died in their twenties and thirties, long before they thought they had to worry about Social Security.

In 1990, 76 million American workers participated in 870,000 pension plans through their employers. Employer contributions to these plans make up a significant part of the total compensation for these workers, who count on the resulting benefits to produce an average of 34 percent of their retirement incomes. Yet 25 million workers will never collect a cent from the pension plans in which they are currently enrolled.

Despite the importance of Social Security and pension programs to nearly every American worker, few bother to pay attention until retirement nears. The result is that millions of Americans are either deprived of benefits or receive less in benefits than they have earned because they failed to protect these benefits during their working years. Millions of others at or beyond retirement age lose vital income because they don't know how to appeal unfavorable decisions and defend their rights.

That's why the information in *Protect Your Social Security, Medicare, and Pension Benefits* is vital for every American from the youngest working age through his or her retirement years. In this book, we explain:

- The details of all Social Security and Medicare programs
- How to apply for Social Security and Medicare
- How to appeal decisions and defend your rights
- How to obtain free or low-cost legal assistance
- How to understand and evaluate your pension plan
- How to defend your pension rights

In addition, this book contains forms that you can use to obtain:

- A record of all your Social Security earnings
- A personal estimate of the Social Security benefits you have earned
- A record of the pension benefits you have earned

Finally, we explain how to use information about your Social Security, Medicare, and pension benefits to formulate a retirement plan that will provide you with the income to enjoy life to the fullest in your later years.

PART I:

PROTECT YOUR SOCIAL SECURITY AND MEDICARE BENEFITS

Your Guide to Social Security Benefits

More than 38 million Americans, including 98 percent of those who are retired, currently receive monthly Social Security checks. If you are working or have worked, Social Security provides you with three types of benefits:

1. Retirement benefits for you as well as for your spouse and dependent children
2. Disability benefits if you are unable to work as well as benefits for your spouse and dependent children
3. Survivor benefits after your death for your spouse, children who are minors (that is, under age 18), disabled older children, and dependent elderly parents

YOU EARN YOUR SOCIAL SECURITY BENEFITS

The most important thing to remember about Social Security is that your benefits are based directly on your earnings from employment and self-employment (and the earnings of your spouse, if you are or have been married). Your earnings are recorded in two separate ways:

1. The number of years, or portions of years, in which you earned money determines your eligibility for all Social Security benefits.
2. The amount of money you have earned over your working life determines the amount of the monthly benefits you and/or your dependents will receive.

YOUR SOCIAL SECURITY DEDUCTION IS IMPORTANT

The Social Security Administration is only able to record your earnings from two sources:

1. The quarterly report of your gross earnings and your Social Security deductions submitted by your employer
2. Your net self-employment earnings and Social Security tax paid as listed on IRS Schedule SE, which you submit annually with your federal income tax return

If all of your earnings aren't reported accurately, you might receive benefits lower than those you've earned or, even worse, you may lose your eligibility to receive benefits at all.

YOUR ELIGIBILITY FOR BENEFITS

You become eligible for Social Security by accumulating *work credits*. You can earn a work credit by earning a certain amount of money during a calendar year, up to a maximum of four work credits for each year. If you worked in 1990, you received one work credit for every $520 (gross pay) you earned. If you earned $2,080 in 1990, you received the maximum four credits.

Because of the relatively small amount of earnings necessary to earn a work credit, it is very important that your wages from even short-term, part-time jobs be reported accurately to the Social Security Administration. All credits you earn become a permanent part of your record, even if you stop working for decades.

YOUR MONTHLY BENEFITS

The amount of the monthly benefits you receive when you retire or become disabled, as well as the survivor benefits paid to your spouse or dependent children, depends on your average annual earnings over your entire working career, up to an annual maximum wage. That maximum wage was $3,000 from 1937 to 1950; then it rose gradually, to $4,800 in 1960, $7,800 in 1970, $25,900 in 1980, and $51,300 in 1990. Future increases will either be established by an act of Congress or will come automatically in a formula tied to the cost-of-living increases in Social Security benefits.

The range of monthly payments from minimum to maximum is quite wide. For example, in 1989 retirement benefits paid to a worker who began collecting at age 65 ranged from a minimum of $465 to a maximum of $975 per month. Any omissions in earnings from your Social Security records could cost you a great deal of money in the future.

YOUR SOCIAL SECURITY RETIREMENT BENEFITS

If you will turn 62 before the year 2000, you can collect:

- Reduced benefits beginning at age 62
- Full benefits at age 65
- Increased benefits for each year worked between age 65 and 69

Beginning in the year 2000, the minimum age for obtaining full benefits will rise gradually from 65 to 67, as shown in the following table:

THE MINIMUM AGE FOR OBTAINING FULL SOCIAL SECURITY BENEFITS

YEAR OF BIRTH	NORMAL RETIREMENT AGE*
1937 or earlier	65
1938	65 and 2 months
1939	65 and 4 months
1940	65 and 6 months
1941	65 and 8 months
1942	65 and 10 months
1943–1954	66
1955	66 and 2 months
1956	66 and 4 months
1957	66 and 6 months
1958	66 and 8 months
1959	66 and 10 months
1960 and later	67

*Normal retirement age is the earliest age at which unreduced retirement benefits can be received.

The minimum age for collecting reduced benefits, however, will not rise.

If you begin to collect Social Security when you reach full retirement age, the amount of your monthly payment will be determined by a complex formula based on your average annual earnings over your working years. In Chapter 2, we tell you how to obtain an estimate of the retirement benefits, based on your past and projected future earnings, that you would receive. You can get a general idea of how much to expect, however, from the table on the following page.

If you choose to retire before the minimum age for obtaining full benefits, your monthly payment will be permanently reduced by 1/180 for every month you are under the minimum age. For example, suppose you retire the month you turn 63 and your full retirement benefit would be $900 per month. Your benefit will be reduced as follows:

$$24 \text{ months} \times 1/180 \times \$900 = \$120 \text{ per month reduction}$$

In other words, you would receive a monthly check for $780 instead of $900.

APPROXIMATE MONTHLY RETIREMENT BENEFITS IF THE WORKER RETIRES AT NORMAL RETIREMENT AGE AND HAD STEADY LIFETIME EARNINGS

WORKER'S AGE IN 1990		Retired Worker's Earnings in 1989								
		$10,000	$15,000	$20,000	$25,000	$30,000	$35,000	$40,000	$45,000	$48,000 +
25	Retired worker only	$648	$830	$1,013	$1,196	$1,296	$1,381	$1,467	$1,553	$1,604
	Worker and spouse	972	1,245	1,519	1,794	1,944	2,071	2,200	2,329	2,406
	Final year earnings	13,700	20,550	27,400	34,250	41,100	47,950	54,800	61,650	65,760
	Replacement rate	57%	48%	44%	42%	38%	35%	32%	30%	29%
35	Retired worker only	599	767	935	1,098	1,199	1,289	1,357	1,436	1,484
	Worker and spouse	898	1,150	1,402	1,647	1,798	1,933	2,035	2,154	2,226
	Final year earnings	12,700	19,050	25,400	31,750	38,100	44,450	50,800	57,150	60,960
	Replacement rate	57%	48%	44%	41%	38%	35%	32%	30%	29%
45	Retired worker only	547	700	852	1,006	1,101	1,168	1,234	1,296	1,332
	Worker and spouse	820	1,050	1,278	1,509	1,651	1,752	1,851	1,944	1,998
	Final year earnings	11,700	17,550	23,400	29,250	35,100	40,950	46,800	52,650	56,160
	Replacement rate	56%	48%	44%	41%	38%	34%	32%	30%	28%
55	Retired worker only	496	632	771	906	986	1,027	1,071	1,107	1,126
	Worker and spouse	744	948	1,156	1,359	1,479	1,540	1,606	1,661	1,689
	Final year earnings	10,700	16,050	21,400	26,750	32,100	37,450	42,800	48,150	51,360
	Replacement rate	56%	47%	43%	41%	37%	33%	30%	28%	26%
65	Retired worker only	456	582	708	832	896	925	946	965	975
	Worker and spouse	684	873	1,062	1,248	1,344	1,387	1,419	1,447	1,463
	Final year earnings	10,000	15,000	20,000	25,000	30,000	35,000	40,000	45,000	48,000
	Replacement rate	55%	47%	42%	40%	36%	32%	28%	26%	24%

Note: *Replacement rate* is the percentage of the final year's earnings that will be replaced by Social Security benefits.

On the other hand, the Social Security laws provide a financial incentive if you decide to continue working for one or more years between the minimum age for collecting full benefits and the time you turn 70. For example, if you are over age 65 in 1991 and are still working, your monthly check will be 3.5 percent higher when you retire. If your full retirement check would be $900 per month, this one extra year of work would permanently earn you $31.50 per month more.

The incentive for working beyond the minimum retirement age will steadily increase in future years, as shown in the following table:

DELAYED RETIREMENT CREDIT RATES		
ATTAIN AGE 65	MONTHLY PERCENTAGE	YEARLY PERCENTAGE
Prior to 1982	1/12 of 1%	1.0%
1982–1989	1/4 of 1%	3.0%
1990–1991	7/24 of 1%	3.5%
1992–1993	1/3 of 1%	4.0%
1994–1995	3/8 of 1%	4.5%
1996–1997	5/12 of 1%	5.0%
1998–1999	11/24 of 1%	5.5%
2000–2001	1/2 of 1%	6.0%
2002–2003	13/24 of 1%	6.5%
2004–2005	7/12 of 1%	7.0%
2006–2007	5/8 of 1%	7.5%
2008 or later	2/3 of 1%	8.0%

Retirement Benefits for Your Spouse and Other Dependents

Other dependents eligible to collect benefits based on your retirement income can begin to collect reduced benefits at age 62. Increased benefits will be paid for work credits you have earned for up to five years after the age for full benefits.

When you retire, your dependents can collect:

• Spouse: 50 percent of your benefit at age 65, or earlier if

caring for a child under 16 or disabled; or a reduced benefit
at age 62
- Children: 50 percent if under age 18 or if older and disabled
- Divorced spouse: 50 percent of your benefit at age 65; or
reduced benefit at age 62, if the marriage lasted 10 years or
more
- Grandchildren: 50 percent of your benefit if under 18 and
living in your home and you provide over half of their
support

How You and Your Dependents Qualify for Retirement Benefits

If you reach age 62 in 1991 or later, you must have accumu-
lated 40 work credits to become fully insured for retirement
benefits. That's working one quarter of every year between
age 21 and age 62. Once you've earned those 40 quarters, you
are permanently eligible for Social Security retirement benefits, even if you haven't worked in years.

How Work Affects Your Social Security Retirement Benefits

Retirement need not mean never working again. Recipients
age 70 and over can earn an unlimited amount of money
without a reduction in their benefits. In 1990, recipients under
age 65 could receive a maximum of $6,840 in salary or self-
employment net income without a reduction in their Social
Security benefits. Above $6,840, they lose $1 in benefits for
each $2 of earned income. In 1990, recipients ages 65 to 69
could receive a maximum of $9,360 in salary or self-employ-
ment income without a reduction in their Social Security
benefits. Above $9,360, they lose $1 in benefits for every $3 of
earned income.

Note: Income from savings, investments, pensions, or insurance does not reduce Social Security benefits.

Are Social Security Benefits Taxable?

Up to 50 percent of your benefits may be taxed on your federal income tax return if your income exceeds a certain amount. On 1990 returns, your benefits were taxed if your adjusted gross income exceeded $25,000 if you were single, or $32,000 if you were married and filed jointly.

Note: Tax-exempt income, such as interest from municipal bonds, is added to your taxable income when the federal taxability of your Social Security benefits is computed.

Many states that have income tax *do not* levy tax on the portion of Social Security benefits that are federally taxed. For specific information on your state, call your state taxpayer information number (see your telephone directory under your state government listing).

YOUR DISABILITY BENEFITS

To receive Social Security disability benefits, you must have a physical or mental impairment that prevents you from holding any substantial gainful employment for a continuous period of at least 12 months or a physical condition that can be expected to end in death. Being unable to work in your previous job is not enough to qualify you for these benefits. For example, you may have a physical condition that prevents you from returning to your job as a carpenter but is not severe enough to prevent you from holding a less strenuous job. Thus you can't collect Social Security disability payments, even if you're unable to find a less strenuous job in your area. You may also be denied disability benefits if you refuse to take part in free vocational rehabilitation programs offered by your state.

The amount of your disability benefits is based on the average amount you have earned in the years before your disability. In Chapter 2, we explain how you can get an estimate of the disability benefits you have earned based on your actual past and projected future earnings. The following table, however, will give you a general idea of the benefits you and your family could expect:

APPROXIMATE MONTHLY RETIREMENT BENEFITS IF THE WORKER BECOMES DISABLED IN 1990 AND HAD STEADY EARNINGS

WORKER'S AGE		Disabled Worker's Earnings in 1989								
		$10,000	$15,000	$20,000	$25,000	$30,000	$35,000	$40,000	$45,000	$48,000 +
25	Disabled worker only	$463	$591	$719	$848	$932	$992	$1,052	$1,112	$1,149
	Disabled worker, spouse, and child	681	887	1,079	1,272	1,398	1,488	1,578	1,668	1,724
35	Disabled worker only	459	586	712	839	926	986	1,045	1,096	1,122
	Disabled worker, spouse, and child	672	879	1,069	1,258	1,390	1,479	1,568	1,645	1,683
45	Disabled worker only	458	585	711	837	923	969	1,004	1,033	1,048
	Disabled worker, spouse, and child	670	877	1,067	1,256	1,384	1,454	1,506	1,550	1,573
55	Disabled worker only	458	584	710	834	905	937	960	980	990
	Disabled worker, spouse, and child	669	877	1,066	1,251	1,358	1,406	1,440	1,471	1,486
64	Disabled worker only	449	573	697	819	882	910	930	948	957
	Disabled worker, spouse, and child	658	860	1,046	1,228	1,323	1,365	1,395	1,422	1,435

Disability and Medicare

You will be eligible for Medicare hospital insurance protection after you have been receiving disability benefits for 24 months. You may also elect to enroll in the Medicare medical insurance program, for which a monthly fee is charged.

Disability Benefits for Your Dependents

Disability benefits based on your earnings could also be payable to:

- Widows or widowers ages 50 to 64 who become disabled within seven years of the death of their spouse
- Children of workers who become disabled before age 22

How You Become Eligible for Disability Benefits

To qualify for benefits if you become disabled, you must have worked long enough and recently enough to qualify. The exact requirements depend on your age at the time you become disabled:

- If you are under age 24, you must have earned six work credits in the preceding three years.
- If you are in the 24-to-30 age group, you must have earned two work credits for every year between age 21 and the age at which you become disabled. For example, if you become disabled at age 28, you must have earned 14 credits in the previous seven years.
- If you are age 31 or older, you must have earned at least 20 work credits during the 10 years before the onset of your disability. In addition, you must have earned the following total credits during your working career:

WORK CREDITS NEEDED TO QUALIFY FOR DISABILITY BENEFITS

BORN AFTER 1929; BECOME DISABLED AT AGE	BORN BEFORE 1930; BECOME DISABLED BEFORE 62 IN	WORK CREDITS NEEDED
31 through 42		20
44		22
46		24
48		26
50		28
52		30
53		31
54		32
55		33
56		34
57	1986	35
58	1987	36
59	1988	37
60	1989	38
62 or older	1991 or later	40

Exception: If you are disabled by blindness, the required credits may have been earned at any time after 1936; you need no recent credit.

What Happens When You Want to Return to Work

Social Security regulations allow you to continue receiving disability benefits for a nine-month trial period during which you test your ability to work. The months do not have to be consecutive. If you're able to continue to work at the end of the trial period, your benefits continue for three months before ceasing.

You also have special protection for three years after your trial period is over. During this period, you're eligible to receive disability benefits for any months you're unable to work simply by notifying your Social Security office.

A third benefit when you return to work is that your Medicare coverage can continue for 39 months after the trial work period.

APPROXIMATE MONTHLY SURVIVOR BENEFITS IF THE WORKER DIES IN 1990 AND HAD STEADY EARNINGS

WORKER'S AGE		Deceased Worker's Earnings in 1989								
		$10,000	$15,000	$20,000	$25,000	$30,000	$35,000	$40,000	$45,000	$48,000 +
25	Spouse and 1 child	$698	$892	$1,086	$1,280	$1,402	$1,494	$1,584	$1,676	$1,736
	Spouse and 2 children	711	1,063	1,321	1,495	1,636	1,742	1,849	1,955	2,026
	1 child only	349	446	543	640	701	747	792	838	868
	Spouse at age 60	332	425	518	610	668	712	755	799	828
35	Spouse and 1 child	688	878	1,070	1,260	1,370	1,480	1,568	1,658	1,712
	Spouse and 2 children	695	1,040	1,306	1,476	1,622	1,726	1,830	1,934	1,996
	1 child only	344	439	535	630	695	740	784	829	856
	Spouse at age 60	328	419	510	600	663	705	748	790	816
45	Spouse and 1 child	688	876	1,066	1,256	1,386	1,460	1,514	1,562	1,586
	Spouse and 2 children	693	1,036	1,303	1,472	1,617	1,703	1,767	1,822	1,849
	1 child only	344	438	533	628	693	730	757	781	793
	Spouse at age 60	328	418	508	599	661	696	722	744	756
55	Spouse and 1 child	686	876	1,066	1,300	1,358	1,406	1,440	1,470	1,486
	Spouse and 2 children	692	1,035	1,302	1,468	1,584	1,639	1,680	1,715	1,733
	1 child only	343	438	533	625	679	703	720	735	743
	Spouse at age 60	327	418	508	596	647	670	686	701	708
65	Spouse and 1 child	684	872	1,062	1,248	1,344	1,386	1,420	1,448	1,462
	Spouse and 2 children	692	1,036	1,295	1,461	1,567	1,618	1,656	1,689	1,705
	1 child only	342	436	531	624	672	693	710	724	731
	Spouse at age 60	326	416	506	595	640	661	676	690	697

SURVIVOR BENEFITS FOR YOUR DEPENDENTS

If you die, your dependents can collect the following percentages of the retirement benefits you were receiving or would have received upon retirement:

- Spouse: 100 percent of your retirement benefit at age 65; a reduced benefit at age 60; 75 percent of benefit at any age if caring for a disabled child
- Children: 75 percent of benefit if under 18 or disabled
- Divorced spouse: Same as spouse, if the marriage lasted 10 years or more
- Parents: Can receive benefits if over 62 and dependent upon you for over half their support

In Chapter 2, we explain how you can obtain an estimate of the survivor benefits your family would receive based on your actual past and projected future earnings. You can get a general idea, however, from the preceding table.

In addition to monthly benefits, your surviving spouse or other dependent (if your spouse is deceased) can receive a one-time, lump-sum death benefit payment of $255 if you have earned sufficient work credits to be eligible for survivor benefits.

How Your Dependents Qualify for Survivor Benefits

Survivor benefits can only be paid to your family if, at the time of your death, you have earned the minimum number of work credits shown in the table on the following page.

Under a special rule, survivor benefits can be paid to your children and your surviving spouse if you have earned six credits in the three years before your death, even if your total work credits fall below the minimum for your age.

WORK CREDITS NEEDED TO QUALIFY FOR SURVIVOR BENEFITS

BORN AFTER 1929; DIE AT AGE	BORN BEFORE 1930; DIE BEFORE 62 IN	WORK CREDITS NEEDED
28 or younger		6
30		8
32		10
34		12
36		14
38		16
40		18
42		20
44		22
46		24
48		26
50		28
52		30
53		31
54		32
55		33
56	1985	34
57	1986	35
58	1987	36
59	1988	37
60	1989	38
61	1990	39
62	1991 or later	40

SOCIAL SECURITY—AN INVALUABLE PACKAGE OF PROTECTION

Social Security retirement, disability, and survivor benefits provide a package of protection that would cost the average American family more than $500 a month in premiums to replace with insurance coverage from private companies. Because of its value and because you earn this coverage through your Social Security taxes, you owe it to yourself and your family to protect every cent in benefits to which you are entitled. Beginning in Chapter 2, we will show you exactly how to do that.

═ 2 ═

How to Obtain a Statement of Your Social Security Earnings and an Estimate of Your Benefits

Since 1988, the Social Security Administration has provided a service invaluable to every American who is working or has worked. Upon submission of a simple form, the SSA will send you a complete year-by-year record of your earnings, Social Security deductions, and work credits. At the same time, the SSA provides you with a customized estimate of the retirement, disability, and survivor benefits you and your family have earned.

You should take advantage of this service at least every three years, for two very important reasons.

First of all, the Social Security benefits described in Chapter 1 provide vital protection for you and your family while you're working and after you retire. That protection, however, depends on the accuracy of the Social Security Administration's records of your work and earning history.

For very understandable reasons, the Social Security records of many Americans contain errors and omissions. The Social Security Administration maintains more than 270 million separate files and must annually record almost $400 billion in Social Security taxes. It is inevitable that mistakes are made:

• By workers, who may provide an employer with the wrong Social Security number or who fail to inform the Social Security Administration that they've changed their names
• By employers, who submit paperwork with the wrong Social Security numbers, misspelled names, or errors in the computation of total earnings and Social Security deductions
• By the Social Security Administration, by entering data inaccurately into the computer

The combination of these types of errors has resulted in the Social Security Administration's holding more than $80 billion in Social Security taxes that it can't credit to the appropriate workers. Some of that money might well be yours. Experts also estimate that tens of billions of dollars in Social Security taxes don't reach the U.S. Treasury at all because employers pay workers "off the books," file incomplete wage statements, or fail to file at all. These omissions might very well result in severe financial hardship for you and your family.

Second, you must know approximately what Social Security benefits you have earned in order to plan adequately for financial emergencies, such as your death or disability, and for retirement. For example, Social Security retirement payments may replace as little as one-fourth of your current income when you retire. Knowing exactly how much you'll be getting in Social Security benefits allows you to meet your future needs by investing additional funds in retirement accounts.

HOW TO FILL OUT THE REQUEST FOR EARNINGS AND BENEFIT ESTIMATE STATEMENT

Form SSA-7004, the Request for Earnings and Benefit Estimate Statement, is included in this book between pages 26 and 27. If you need additional forms for your spouse, parents, children, or others, you can obtain them by using one of the following methods:

- Visit your local Social Security office (see your telephone directory under the United States Government listings).
- Call the Social Security Teleservice toll-free at (800) 234-5772.
- Write the Consumer Information Center, PO Box 100, Pueblo, CO 81002.

When you sit down to fill out the form, you will need:

- Your Social Security card
- A copy of your federal income tax return from the previous year
- A recent pay stub or, if self-employed, your business records

Completing Form SSA-7004 requires you to answer 10 questions:

1. "Name shown on your Social Security card." You should write the name on your current card, even if you have changed your name because of marriage or for another reason. To obtain a new card with your current name:

- Visit or call your local Social Security office.
- Call Social Security Teleservice toll-free at (800) 234-5772.

If you have lost your Social Security card, you can obtain a new card in the same way.

2. "Your Social Security number as shown on your card." Make sure to copy this number accurately. Check your pay stub and tax return to ensure that those documents include the right number.

3. "Your date of birth." You will normally need to submit a copy of your birth certificate when applying for Social Security benefits, so be sure to provide your correct birth date.

4. "Other Social Security numbers you may have used." You may have applied for a new Social Security number and card after changing your name, after losing your previous Social Security card, or for another reason. Your earnings record will be complete only if you provide those other numbers.

5. "Your Sex."

6. "Other names you have used (including a maiden name)." One of the most common reasons why earnings and Social Security deductions are inaccurately recorded is that the holder of a Social Security number has used two or more names. It is important that you list your maiden name, name from a previous marriage, a stage or professional name, or any other name or nickname you have used, including nicknames for your first name.

7. "Show your actual earnings for last year and your estimated earnings for this year." For Social Security purposes, "earnings" means only wages and net income from self-employment. Do not include interest income, dividends, capital gains, investment income, pensions, insurance payments, or other nonearned income.

A. "Last year's actual earnings." Using your previous year's income tax form, you should write down the total of:

• Wages, salaries, and tips from Form 1040, line 7; Form 1040A, line 7; or Form 1040EZ, line 1
• Net self-employment income from Schedule SE, line 7, if self-employed

B. "This year's estimated earnings." Use your pay stub and, if self-employed, your business records to estimate what you will earn this year.

8. "Show the age at which you plan to retire." If you don't know or haven't decided when you will retire, you should show the age at which you'll be eligible for full retirement benefits (see Chapter 1).

9. "Your future average annual earnings." The Social Security Administration suggests that most people enter the same amount as this year's estimated earnings (question 7B). The reason is that your benefit estimate will be in current dollars (eliminating inflation as a consideration) and that your benefit estimate will be calculated to include the average annual wage increase over the national economy.

You should enter a different figure only if you know your income will be significantly higher or lower in future years. For example, you may be planning to return to work full-time when your children are out of school, to make a career change, to move to a part of the country where wages are lower, to open your own business, or to switch from full-time to part-time work. However, don't spend a lot of time doing complex calculations or worrying about this figure. If you have to apply for benefits in the future, they will be based on what you have actually earned rather than on your current estimate of future earnings. As your income changes, you can obtain additional estimate statements by submitting SSA-7004 forms in future years.

10. "Address where you want us to send the statement." You may choose to have the statement sent to your accountant, financial planner, or other professional. This address does not have to be your permanent residence. It does, however, have to be an address where the statement can be received in four to six weeks.

When you're finished answering the 10 questions, make sure to sign and date the SSA-7004 form and provide a daytime telephone number (in case problems arise such as illegible handwriting and incomplete answers). It's a good idea to make a photocopy of the form and put it away in a file with copies of any notes or records you've used in preparing it.

Mail the form (between pages 26 and 27) to the following address:
Social Security Administration
Wilkes-Barre Data Operations Center
PO Box 20
Wilkes-Barre, PA 18703

You should receive your statement in six weeks or less.

HOW TO VERIFY AND USE YOUR PERSONAL EARNINGS AND BENEFIT STATEMENT

About four to six weeks after you send in the SSA-7004, you will receive in the mail your Personal Earnings and Benefit Statement. You should set aside a block of time to verify carefully the information it contains and to evaluate the benefit estimates.

The Personal Earnings and Benefit Statement contains the following sections:

"The Facts You Gave Us"

Included in this first section are:

Your name
Your Social Security number
Your date of birth
Previous year's earnings
This year's estimated earnings
Your estimated future average yearly earnings
The age you plan to retire

You should compare this information with the photocopy you made of the SSA-7004 form you submitted. If any errors were made by Social Security in entering the information, call (800) 937-7005.

"Your Social Security Earnings"

This section, by far the most important part of the entire statement, provides the following information for every year since 1937:

1. Maximum Yearly Earnings Subject to Social Security Tax (Column 1). This figure represents the maximum amount of earnings from wages, salaries, and self-employment that is subject to Social Security tax. For example, in 1989 the figure was $48,000.

2. Your Social Security Taxed Earnings (Column 2). This figure represents Social Security's official record of the amount of your earned income that was subject to Social Security tax. The Social Security Administration records your earnings only up to the maximum yearly earnings subject to Social Security tax. For example, you may have earned $60,000 in 1989, but your Personal Earnings and Benefit Statement will show only $48,000, the maximum subject to Social Security tax.

Note: It takes Social Security more than a year to record information from income tax returns and statements submitted by employers. For that reason, you may see the phrase "Not Yet Posted" for information from the previous year.

3. Estimated Social Security Taxes You Paid (Column 3). This figure represents the Social Security taxes that were deducted from your paychecks or that you paid directly if you were self-employed.

Take a moment to look over your earnings record. If your Social Security taxed earnings equaled the maximum yearly earnings throughout your career, you know you are entitled to the maximum possible benefits, and you can move on to the rest of this statement.

Many of you, however, will find that your Social Security taxed earnings didn't reach the maximum in one or more years. *It is vital that you find out if all of your earnings for those years were accurately recorded.*

To verify your earnings, you will need a copy of your federal income tax return for every year in question. If you do not have your returns for one or more years, you can obtain copies from the Internal Revenue Service by filing Form 4506, the Request for Copy of Tax form.

You can obtain a copy of this form from:

- Your local IRS office (see your telephone directory under the United States Government listings)
- Your local library (the IRS distributes complete sets of reproducible forms to 18,000 public libraries)
- By mail from one of the following addresses:

If you live in Connecticut, Delaware, the District of Columbia, Florida, Georgia, Maine, Maryland, Massachusetts, New Hampshire, New Jersey, New York, North Carolina, Pennsylvania, Rhode Island, South Carolina, Vermont, Virginia, West Virginia:

Forms Distribution Center
PO Box 25866
Richmond, VA 23289

If you live in Alabama, Arkansas, Illinois, Indiana, Iowa, Kansas, Kentucky, Louisiana, Michigan, Minnesota, Mississippi, Missouri, Nebraska, North Dakota, Ohio, Oklahoma, South Dakota, Tennessee, Texas, Wisconsin:

Forms Distribution Center
PO Box 9903
Bloomington, IL 61799

If you live in Alaska, Arizona, California, Colorado, Hawaii, Idaho, Montana, Nevada, New Mexico, Oregon, Utah, Washington, Wyoming:

Forms Distribution Center
Rancho Cordova, CA 95743-0001

SOCIAL SECURITY ADMINISTRATION

Request for Earnings and Benefit Estimate Statement

To receive a free statement of your earnings covered by Social Security and your estimated future benefits, all you need to do is fill out this form. Please print or type your answers. When you have completed the form, fold it and mail it to us.

1. Name shown on your Social Security card:

    _____
    First   Middle Initial   Last

2. Your Social Security number as shown on your card:

    ☐ ☐ ☐ – ☐ ☐ – ☐ ☐ ☐ ☐

3. Your date of birth: _____   _____   _____
    Month   Day   Year

4. Other Social Security numbers you may have used:

    ☐ ☐ ☐ – ☐ ☐ – ☐ ☐ ☐ ☐

    ☐ ☐ ☐ – ☐ ☐ – ☐ ☐ ☐ ☐

5. Your Sex: ☐ Male   ☐ Female

6. Other names you have used (including a maiden name):

    _____

    _____

7. Show your actual earnings for last year and your estimated earnings for this year. Include only wages and/or net self-employment income subject to Social Security tax.

    A. Last year's actual earnings:

        $ ☐ ☐ ☐ , ☐ ☐ ☐ . ⓪ ⓪
           Dollars only

    B. This year's estimated earnings:

        $ ☐ ☐ ☐ , ☐ ☐ ☐ . ⓪ ⓪
           Dollars only

8. Show the age at which you plan to retire: _____

Form SSA-7004-PC-OP1 (6/88) DESTROY PRIOR EDITIONS

9. Below, show an amount which you think best represents your future average yearly earnings between now and when you plan to retire. The amount should be a yearly average, not your total future lifetime earnings. Only show earnings subject to Social Security tax.

Most people should enter the same amount as this year's estimated earnings (the amount shown in 7B). The reason for this is that we will show your retirement benefit estimate in today's dollars, but adjusted to account for average wage growth in the national economy.

However, if you expect to earn significantly more or less in the future than what you currently earn because of promotions, a job change, part-time work, or an absence from the work force, enter the amount in today's dollars that will most closely reflect your future average yearly earnings. Do not add in cost-of-living, performance, or scheduled pay increases or bonuses.

Your future average yearly earnings:

$ ☐☐☐,☐☐☐.⟮0⟯⟮0⟯
  Dollars only

10. Address where you want us to send the statement:

_____
Name

_____
Street Address (Include Apt. No., P.O. Box, or Rural Route)

_____
City   State   Zip Code

I am asking for information about my own Social Security record or the record of a person I am authorized to represent. I understand that if I deliberately request information under false pretenses I may be guilty of a federal crime and could be fined and/or imprisoned. I authorize you to send the statement of my earnings and benefit estimates to me or my representative through a contractor.

▶

_____
Please sign your name (Do not print)

_____
Date   (Area Code) Daytime Telephone No.

☐ SP

You will have to pay a small fee for every tax return.

When you have copies of your tax returns, sit down and compare your earnings from each year's form with the entries in Column 2, Your Social Security Taxed Earnings. If you filed an individual tax return for the year in question, your earnings are the total of the wages, salaries, and tips listed plus any self-employment net income listed on Schedule SE. If you filed a joint return, you will have to use the W-2 forms to separate your income from that of your spouse.

When you are finished, make a list of any errors that you find. How to correct those errors is explained in Chapter 3.

"Your Social Security Credits"

As was explained in Chapter 1, you need a certain number of work credits to qualify for Social Security benefits. The last sentence of this section tells you how many credits you have earned, based on the earnings statement above. Correcting errors in the earning statement will adjust your credit total.

"Estimated Benefits—Retirement"

This section provides three pieces of information:

1. The earliest age at which you can retire with unreduced benefits
2. The monthly benefit, in today's dollars, which you could expect to receive at that age
3. The monthly benefit you would receive if you worked until age 70

"Estimated Benefits—Survivors"

This section contains five pieces of information:

1. The number of credits you need for your family members to receive benefits if you were to die this year

2. The monthly benefit to your child if you were to die this year
3. The monthly benefit your child and spouse would each receive
4. The monthly benefit your spouse would receive when he or she reached full retirement age
5. The one-time, lump-sum death benefit payment your spouse or children would receive

"Estimated Benefits—Disability"

This section contains three pieces of information:

1. The number of credits you need to be insured for disability should you become disabled this year
2. Your monthly benefit should you become disabled
3. The maximum monthly benefit you and your family could receive should you become disabled

These estimates are critical to your financial planning for emergencies and for retirement. For example, your estimated Social Security retirement benefit plus your estimated pension benefit (which you can obtain by following the instructions in Chapter 9) are the basis of your retirement income. By comparing these figures with your estimates of your expenses during retirement, you will know how much income you will need to generate from retirement savings and investments.

═ 3 ═

How to Correct Errors in Your Social Security Records

It is so important that your Social Security earnings records be accurate that the U.S. Congress recently enacted legislation eliminating any time limit for correcting errors. The longer you wait to verify your records, however, the more difficult it is to assemble evidence to correct any errors. You should still review your records at least once every three years to detect errors caused by:

- *Employer fraud.* For example, your employer may have pocketed your Social Security deduction instead of reporting it.
- *Mechanical or clerical error.* If someone punched the wrong key while entering your records into a computer, you're entitled to a correction.
- *Funds credited to the wrong person or to a wrong period.* For example, your employer may have submitted your earnings under someone else's Social Security number or with an incorrect date.
- *Employer failing to report wages.* If your employer forgot to report your wages, you aren't penalized.
- *Self-employment income not recorded.* If you filed your income tax return and paid your self-employment Social Security tax on time, the Social Security Administration

must correct your record if this income was not entered accurately.

ASSEMBLING YOUR PROOF OF EARNINGS

Before you contact the Social Security Administration, you should attempt to obtain some proof that you earned the money in question. Among the pieces of evidence that the SSA will accept are:

* A statement of earnings from your employer
* Your Form W-2 (Wage and Tax Statement) for that year
* Pay envelopes or pay stubs showing the dates and the amount of wages paid
* Union records
* State unemployment compensation office records

If none of these records are available, the Social Security Administration will consider other evidence such as your personal statement, your record of bank deposits, or statements from others who have knowledge that you worked. This evidence carries less weight, however, than the more official documents.

PREVENTING FUTURE ERRORS

Trouble locating your past W-2 forms, pay stubs, or other records is evidence that you haven't been diligent about saving important financial records. You can save yourself a lot of time and aggravation in the future by setting up a file for all important wage and earnings documents.

CONTACTING SOCIAL SECURITY

When you have assembled your evidence, you should contact your local Social Security office. You can locate this office by looking in the telephone directory under the United States Government listing or by calling (800) 234-5772. You may want to call first before you go to the office. Simple errors can often be corrected by telephone. If not, you can still make an appointment to save waiting time.

When you notify Social Security that you believe your records contain one or more errors, your local office will institute a computer check to see if the missing funds can be located. This check often uncovers errors such as the transposing of digits in your Social Security number and misspellings of your name. At the same time, your local office may submit for you a Form SSA-7050 (Request for Social Security Earnings Information), which provides more details about your earnings than your Personal Earnings and Benefit Statement.

If your local office can't locate the missing earnings, a letter will be written to your employer. By law, however, the Social Security Administration cannot identify you by name without your permission. If you don't want your employer to know that you've contacted Social Security, your local office will ask the employer for a copy of the report for all wages it has paid to you during the period in question in order to verify your earnings. Frequently, an error in an individual's record is corrected when this report is received.

If a discrepancy in your records is found because your employer has fraudulently or mistakenly failed to report some or all of your earnings, your employer may dispute your claim. In that case, the SSA will conduct an investigation. When the investigation is completed, their decision, known as an *initial determination*, will be issued. If this determination is that you did have additional earnings, they will be credited to your records immediately. If the determination goes against your claim, you are entitled to appeal the decision. For detailed information about your recourses if an initial determination goes against you, see Chapter 5.

═ 4 ═

How to Apply for Social Security Benefits

Social Security benefits are not paid to you automatically—
you must apply for all benefits to which you (and your dependents) are entitled.

APPLYING FOR RETIREMENT BENEFITS

The Social Security Administration recommends that you contact your local Social Security office two to three months before the date you expect to retire. You can apply up to the day before your retirement month to receive benefits immediately. You can also, in some cases, receive retroactive benefits for as long as 12 months. But contacting the SSA early has significant advantages:

- You may avoid delays in receiving Medicare benefits.
- You have more time to locate any additional documents you may need in order to receive benefits. For example, if you don't have a birth certificate, you need to obtain some other acceptable proof of age before benefits can be issued.
- You may learn that delaying your retirement, even for a few months, could increase your lifetime benefits.
- You can initiate your appeals process sooner if your application for benefits is initially denied.

You can apply for retirement benefits either by phone or in person:

- Call the Social Security Teleservice toll-free at (800) 234-5772. You can speak to an operator between 7:00 A.M. and 7:00 P.M. on business days. Other times and days you can leave a message for someone to call you back.
- Visit your local Social Security office (see your telephone directory under the United States Government listings).

If it is necessary for you to see a Social Security representative in person and your health makes it difficult for you to travel, you can make an appointment for a home visit.

When you apply for Social Security benefits, you should have the following documents:

- Your birth certificate
- Your Social Security card or another document that shows your number
- Evidence of your recent earnings, such as last year's W-2 forms or self-employment income tax return

If you are applying for benefits as a spouse, you should also have:

- Your marriage certificate or other proof of marriage
- Your divorce certificate (if applicable)

If you are applying for benefits for a dependent or disabled child, you should have:

- The child's birth certificate
- Adoption papers (if applicable)

One very important point to remember: *Do not delay applying for Social Security benefits if you don't have one or more of these documents.* Your local Social Security office will help you obtain missing documents or suggest other acceptable proofs. Once again, the earlier you start, the more likely you are to receive your monthly benefits when you want them.

APPLYING FOR SURVIVOR BENEFITS

You should apply for survivor benefits and the $255 lump-sum death benefit as soon as possible after a worker's death either by phone or in person:

• Call the Social Security Teleservice toll-free at (800) 234-5772. You can speak to an operator between 7:00 A.M. and 7:00 P.M. on business days. Other times and days you can leave a message for someone to call you back.
• Visit your local Social Security office (see your telephone directory under the United States Government listings).

  The Social Security Administration will need certain evidence to complete your application:

• Your Social Security number and the deceased worker's number
• Your birth certificate or other proof of age
• The deceased worker's W-2 forms or self-employment tax returns from the previous year
• The worker's death certificate or other proof of death
• Your marriage certificate or other proof of marriage, if you are the surviving spouse
• Your divorce papers, if you are applying as a divorced widow or widower
• The birth certificates and Social Security numbers of any children applying for benefits
• Proof that the deceased supported you if you are applying for benefits as a dependent parent or grandchild

  In certain circumstances, Social Security may ask for additional proof or information. You should not delay applying for benefits, however, even if you don't have all the documents you need. Social Security can begin the application process and help you find the proofs you need.

APPLYING FOR DISABILITY BENEFITS

Processing an application for disability benefits takes considerably longer than processing applications for any other type of Social Security benefit. That is why you should apply as soon as you believe that your disability will prevent you from working for a year or more. Payments cannot begin until you have been disabled for at least six months. Back payments may be made for up to 12 months before the application date but cannot go back further than the sixth month of disability.

You can begin the application process either by phone or in person:

- Call the Social Security Teleservice toll-free at (800) 234-5772. You can speak to an operator between 7:00 A.M. and 7:00 P.M. on business days. Other times and days you can leave a message for someone to call you back.
- Visit your local Social Security office (see your telephone directory under the United States Government listings).

Social Security needs a great deal of information to process your claim:

- Your Social Security number as well as the numbers of others (your spouse and dependent children) who will be collecting benefits
- Your birth certificate or other proof of age
- Birth certificates or other proofs of age of others who may be receiving payments
- Names, addresses, and telephone numbers of doctors, hospitals, clinics, and institutions that have treated you, along with the dates of treatment
- A summary of where you have worked in the last 15 years and what types of work you have done

- Your W-2 forms or self-employment tax return for the previous year
- Dates of any military service
- The claim number of any other benefit you receive or expect to receive because of your disability
- Your marriage certificate, if you're applying for benefits for your spouse
- The worker's death certificate, if you're applying as a disabled surviving spouse
- Proof your marriage lasted at least ten years, if you're applying as a disabled surviving divorced spouse

After you file your application, the SSA reviews it to see if you have enough work credits and if you meet other basic requirements to qualify for consideration for benefits. Your application is then sent to the Disability Determination office in your state. There a physician and a disability evaluation specialist will make a decision about whether or not you are considered disabled under the provision of Social Security regulation. During this review, you may be asked to help obtain medical records or even to take a special physical exam (at Social Security's expense). This process normally takes at least two to three months.

IF THE PERSON ELIGIBLE FOR BENEFITS ISN'T COMPETENT TO MANAGE HIS OR HER OWN AFFAIRS

If you are not mentally or physically able to apply for Social Security benefits, your spouse, child, parent, legal guardian, friend, or even the director of an institution to which you're confined may complete the application for you.

However, Social Security provides protection for benefit recipients who may not be capable of managing their own money. Before anyone, even a spouse, can receive and disperse your Social Security benefits, the Social Security Administration must certify that there is convincing evidence that you are incapable of managing your own money. Before designating anyone to receive and disperse your checks as a *representative payee*, Social Security tries to ensure that that person has and will continue to have a strong interest in your welfare and care. Federal law stipulates a maximum prison term of five years and a $25,000 fine for any representative payee who misappropriates or misuses the funds intended for the care of a beneficiary.

ONCE YOUR BENEFITS ARE APPROVED

When your application is approved, you (and each of your dependents, if any) will receive a monthly benefit check. For your safety and convenience, Social Security recommends that you have your money deposited directly into your account at a financial institution. With a little shopping, you should be able to find a bank, savings and loan, or credit union that won't charge you a fee for maintaining an account for receiving your monthly check. Of course, you may also request that your check be mailed to you.

WHEN YOU WILL RECEIVE YOUR CHECK

Social Security checks are usually dated and delivered on the third day of the month following the month for which payment is due. That is, the check for February will be dated and delivered to you on March 3. If the third of the month falls on a Saturday, Sunday, or legal holiday, the checks will be dated and delivered on the last business day before the third. For example, if March 3 falls on a Sunday, all checks will be dated and delivered on Friday, March 1.

If you do not receive your check within three business days after it is due, you should notify Social Security immediately by phone or in person:

• Call Social Security Teleservice toll-free at (800) 234-5772. You can speak to an operator between 7:00 A.M. and 7:00 P.M. on business days. Other times and days you can

leave a message for someone to call you back.
- Visit your local Social Security office (see your telephone directory under the United States Government listings).

If your address changes, you should also notify Social Security immediately in the same manner.

═══ 5 ═══

How to Obtain the Maximum Benefits from Social Security

Making sure that your Social Security earnings records are complete and applying on time for Social Security benefits are two vital steps in insuring that you and your dependents receive the maximum benefits to which you are entitled. The third step you can take is to understand that you have extensive legal rights to challenge any decisions made by Social Security that you believe are wrong or unfair.

As was mentioned before, the volume of paperwork handled by Social Security inevitably produces some clerical or computer errors. In addition, the Social Security representative(s) who handles your claim may misinterpret Social Security regulations or interpret them too harshly. As a result, you may be unhappy with the initial determination of the benefits you receive after you file your application.

Unfortunately, many people lose income and suffer financial hardship by failing to exercise their rights to challenge decisions made by the Social Security Administration. Among the reasons: they are unaware that they can appeal decisions, they feel the appeal process is too complicated or expensive, or they are afraid that challenging a decision will "get them in trouble" with the SSA. The information in this chapter enables you to overcome these and any related concerns you may have.

WHEN YOU CAN CHALLENGE A DECISION

You have the legal right to make use of the review system of the Social Security Administration and the federal judicial system to challenge initial decisions made by the Social Security Administration about any of the following 14 matters:

1. Your right to receive benefits or to continue to receive benefits
2. Your right to resume receiving benefits. For example, your right to resume disability benefits if your disabling condition recurs
3. The amount of benefits you are entitled to receive
4. Any recomputation of benefits
5. Your request for revisions of your earnings record
6. Reduction in your benefits because you worked after retirement
7. Termination of your benefits
8. Any decision that another person should receive your benefit checks because you are determined not capable of managing your financial affairs
9. Any adjustment or recovery because benefits were underpaid or overpaid
10. Recovery of benefits because you received Supplemental Social Security payments or workmen's compensation payments
11. Reduction or termination of disability benefits because you won't participate in vocational rehabilitation programs
12. A decision that your medical condition is not disabling under Social Security regulations
13. A penalty imposed because you failed to report certain information to Social Security
14. Nonpayment of benefits because you were confined to jail for conviction of a felony

Most of the decisions that you are legally unable to challenge involve waivers of Social Security regulations or investigative matters. For example, you cannot appeal Social Security's decision not to extend a time limit mandated by Social Security law (for example, the 60-day limit on requesting a reconsideration of an administrative decision), nor can you appeal Social Security's decision to stop sending your checks to a representative payee while they are investigating possible fraud.

However, these exceptions occur relatively infrequently and should not deter you from beginning the appeals process whenever you feel a decision by Social Security is wrong.

HOW TO CHALLENGE A DECISION BY SOCIAL SECURITY

Social Security provides an established procedure to challenge decisions.

Step 1: Request a Reconsideration

Your first step in challenging a decision is easy. You request that Social Security formally reconsider the decision. You must submit your request *within 60 days after the date of the initial determination*. You can make the request either by mail or in person:

- Fill out a Request for Reconsideration form available at any Social Security office.
- Write a letter to any Social Security office.

Before you submit the form or a letter, it's a good idea to talk to a Social Security representative to ask for an explanation of the initial decision. The explanation may enable you to include additional information or copies of additional documents with your request for a reconsideration.

The reconsideration will be made by an entirely different staff or person than was involved in the initial determination. The people handling reconsiderations are trained to catch and correct common clerical and administrative errors. Many problems are solved at this stage.

Step 2: Request a Hearing Before an Administrative Law Judge

If you disagree with the reconsideration, you have the right to request a hearing before an administrative law judge. *You must apply within 60 days after the date of the reconsideration.* You can request the hearing by filling out a Request for Administrative Hearing form obtained from Social Security or by writing a letter to any Social Security office. The hearing must be scheduled at a location no more than 75 miles from your home. If the hearing is more than 75 miles away, the government will pay for your transportation.

This hearing is your best chance to overturn an unfavorable decision. To prepare for the hearing, you should:

1. Learn more about the Social Security regulations in question. There are a number of excellent resources that can provide you with information on your legal rights to Social Security benefits, including:

▶ Organization: Legal Counsel for the Elderly
 PO Box 96474
 Washington, DC 20090
 Services: This arm of AARP publishes a number of useful publications, including these self-help handbooks:
 Common Sense Guide to Social Security Disability ($3.95)
 Common Sense Guide to Social Security Retirement ($3.95)

▶ Publication: *Tomorrow's Choices: Preparing Now for Future Legal, Financial and Health Care Decisions,* CD134791
 Cost: Free
 From: AARP Fulfillment
 1909 K Street NW
 Washington, DC 20049

▶ Book: *Your Legal Rights Later in Life*, by John Regan
  Cost: $13.95 ($10.35 for AARP members) plus $1.75
    postage
  Contains: A comprehensive 272-page guide to your
    legal rights
  From: AARP Books/Scott, Foresman and Company
        1865 Miner Street
        Des Plaines, IL 60016

▶ Booklet: *Your Rights over Age 50*
  Cost: $3.00
  Contains: An overview of basic rights prepared by the
    American Bar Association. When ordering, ask also
    for a list of other ABA publications.
  From: American Bar Association
        Information Services
        750 North Lake Shore Drive
        Chicago, IL 60611
        (312) 988-5158

▶ Publication: *The Rights of Older Persons*
  Cost: $9.45
  Contains: A comprehensive guide prepared by the
    American Civil Liberties Union
  From: Southern Illinois University Press
        PO Box 3697
        Carbondale, IL 62902

▶ Organization: National Senior Citizen Law Center
        2025 M Street NW, Suite 400
        Washington, DC 20036
        (202) 887-5280
  Services: Provides information on legal rights of older
    Americans in a number of areas

---

2. Ask your Senator or Congressman for help. Your U.S.
Senators and your Congressman were elected to help serve
you. Each of your elected representatives has staff members
assigned specifically to assist constituents with problems in-

volving the federal government, including Social Security. If your request for a reconsideration is denied, you should send a copy of all relevant information to your Senators and your Congressman, with a short cover letter explaining the problem and the solution that you would like. You can obtain the names and addresses of your state's U.S. Senators and your district's U.S. Representative by looking in your telephone directory under the United States Government listings.

3. Consider obtaining the services of an attorney or paralegal professional to represent you. Don't let worries about the cost prevent you from investigating the possibility of retaining a legal professional who could greatly increase your chances of attaining a favorable result from the hearing. First of all, you may be able to get free legal help. In 1987 Congress amended the Older Americans Act to require every state to mandate that each area Agency on Aging set aside a minimum percentage of its funding to provide free legal assistance to older people. To locate your area's Agency on Aging and to obtain other information on free legal services, call your state Agency on Aging at one of the following numbers:

Alabama: (205) 261-5743
Alaska: (907) 465-3250
Arizona: (602) 542-4446
Arkansas: (501) 682-2441
California: (916) 322-5290
Colorado: (303) 866-5905
Connecticut: (203) 566-3238
Delaware: (302) 421-6791
District of Columbia: (202) 724-5622
Florida: (904) 488-8922
Georgia: (404) 894-5333
Hawaii: (808) 548-2593
Idaho: (208) 334-3833
Illinois: (217) 785-2870

Indiana: (317) 232-7000
Iowa: (515) 281-5187
Kansas: (913) 296-4986
Kentucky: (502) 564-6930
Louisiana: (504) 925-1700
Maine: (207) 289-2561
Maryland: (301) 225-1106
Massachusetts: (617) 727-7750
Michigan: (517) 373-8230
Minnesota: (612) 296-2544
Mississippi: (601) 949-2013
Missouri: (314) 751-3082
Montana: (406) 444-5900
Nebraska: (402) 471-2306
Nevada: (702) 885-4210
New Hampshire: (603) 271-4680
New Jersey: (609) 292-4833
New Mexico: (505) 827-7640
New York: (800) 342-9871
North Carolina: (919) 733-3983
North Dakota: (701) 224-2577
Ohio: (614) 466-5500
Oklahoma: (405) 521-2327
Oregon: (503) 378-4728
Pennsylvania: (717) 783-1550
Rhode Island: (401) 277-2858
South Carolina: (803) 783-3203
South Dakota: (605) 773-3656
Tennessee: (615) 741-2056
Texas: (512) 444-2727
Utah: (801) 538-3910
Vermont: (802) 241-2400
Virginia: (804) 225-2271
Washington: (206) 586-3768
West Virginia: (304) 348-3317
Wisconsin: (608) 266-2536
Wyoming: (307) 777-7986

A number of state and local governments, often in cooperation with bar associations and law schools, have developed additional programs to provide legal assistance to older Americans. For a listing of programs such as these in your state, contact:

▶ Organization: American Bar Association
Commission on Legal Problems of the
Elderly
1800 M Street NW
Washington, DC 20036
(202) 331-2297

If you cannot obtain free legal assistance, you may have to hire an attorney. Social Security regulations make this a somewhat less painful process. By federal law, the attorney who represents you must submit his or her fees to the Social Security Administration, which determines if the fees are reasonable. If they are not, your attorney must resubmit a reasonable figure. If they are, Social Security can pay the attorney and deduct the cost from your monthly benefit checks.

While this procedure eases the financial burden of hiring an attorney, it does not ensure the quality of legal services you receive. To obtain a referral to a reputable attorney with significant experience pursuing Social Security claims, you can contact:

▶ Organization: National Organization of Social Security
Claimants' Representatives
Cost: Free referral and brochure
Service: Provides referral to member attorneys who
specialize in Social Security problems
For information: (800) 431-2804 (Except NY)
(914) 735-8812 (In NY)

Before you hire an attorney to represent you at the hearing, ask the attorney to review your records and give you an appraisal of your chances of obtaining a favorable hearing. A reputable lawyer will advise you to save your money if your case is very weak.

At the hearing, you have the right to:

• Appear in person (but you don't have to appear).
• Present new evidence.
• Examine evidence used to make previous decisions.
• Have an attorney or other representative speak for you.
• Call and question witnesses.

Step 3: Request a Review by the Appeals Council

If the result of your hearing before an administrative law judge is unfavorable, you have the right to ask for a review of the case by the Appeals Council, which is also part of the SSA's review system. *You must apply within 60 days of the decision by the administrative law judge.* You can request this review by writing to any Social Security office.

The Appeals Council can refuse to review your case if it does not find that it involves a significant question of Social Security law or administrative policy. In most cases, you should have your request prepared by an attorney who can point out the legal significance of your case.

If the Appeals Council agrees to review your case, you or your attorney can request the opportunity to go to the SSA's headquarters in Washington, D.C., to present oral arguments. The Appeals Council can grant or deny that request. If the request is denied, your case will be decided on the basis of written evidence you submit.

Step 4: Take Your Case to Federal Court

If you are dissatisfied with the decision of the Appeals Council or with its decision not to review your case, you or your attorney can file a civil law suit in a federal district court. *You*

must file within 60 days of the decision by the appeals court.
Your attorney will normally advise you to take this last
recourse only if your case involves major legal issues and a
great deal of money.

Step 5: Have Your Case Reopened or Revised

Even after you have exhausted all your rights to appeal and
the Social Security decision has become final, you have the
right to have the case reopened *within four years of the initial
determination* if you show *good cause*. Good cause generally
means providing new evidence, demonstrating a clerical error,
or bringing evidence of fraud. You can request to have your
case reopened by writing to any Social Security office.

$\equiv$ 6 $\equiv$

Your Guide to Supplemental
Social Security Benefits

Supplemental Social Security Income (SSI) is a program that provides a minimum monthly income to needy Americans who meet one of the following criteria:

• Age 65 or older
• Blind
• Disabled as defined by Social Security regulations

You do not need to have any work credits or earnings to receive SSI benefits, although you can't own much or have much income. SSI is administered through Social Security offices, but benefits are paid from the general revenues of the federal government, not from contributions to the Social Security system. In many states, people who receive federal SSI benefits receive an additional check every month from the state government. Most SSI recipients are also eligible for food stamps, and they can apply for them in Social Security offices at the same time they apply for SSI.

Congress created SSI in 1973 to provide vital support for people who haven't worked much in their lives or who held jobs not covered by Social Security. Unfortunately, a recent federal study showed that less than half of all older Americans eligible for SSI payments had applied for those benefits. For this reason, the American Association of Retired Persons (AARP) has launched a nationwide campaign to reach eligible people who are struggling financially.

WHO IS ELIGIBLE FOR SSI

To receive SSI, aged, blind, or disabled people must prove they have both gross income and assets below a certain level. In 1990, recipients had to have an income below $406 per month for a single person and $599 per month for a couple. Not counted in this income was:

• The first $65 per month you earn working
• Food stamps
• Food, clothing, or shelter you get from nonprofit organizations
• Most home energy assistance

SSI recipients have their benefits reduced by one dollar for every dollar of unearned income they receive, such as pensions or welfare payments. However, as a further incentive to work, their benefits are reduced only one dollar for every two dollars in earned income they receive.

In 1990, recipients had to prove they had liquid assets below $2,000 for a single person and $3,000 for a couple. Social Security defines "liquid assets" as cash or items that could be sold for cash within 20 days such as stocks, bonds, mutual funds, checking accounts, and certain property. However, Social Security does not consider the following items as assets:

• The house you own and live in
• Your household furnishings and personal property with a total value under $2,000
• One wedding ring and one engagement ring
• One automobile, if it is used to provide necessary transportation or if it's worth less than $4,500

- Life insurance policies
- A cemetery plot and money you have set aside to pay for your burial

As with any Social Security program, SSI requirements have scores of exceptions and exclusions too complicated to include here. For example, some recipients can receive both regular Social Security benefits and SSI benefits at the same time. AARP urges all older or disabled people who are struggling financially to contact Social Security about SSI. A large percentage of people who do so find that they are eligible for some benefits.

If You Live in an Institution

Most people who live in city or county rest homes, halfway houses, or other public institutions are not eligible to receive SSI benefits. However, you may be able to receive checks if you live in:

- A publicly operated community residence with 16 residents or less
- An institution where you are living to get approved educational or job training
- A public emergency shelter for the homeless

HOW TO APPLY FOR SSI BENEFITS

You can apply for SSI benefits for yourself or a relative by phone or in person:

- Call the Social Security Teleservice toll-free at (800) 234-5772. You can speak to an operator between 7:00 A.M. and 7:00 P.M. on business days. Other times and days you can leave a message for someone to call you back.
- Visit your local Social Security office (see your telephone directory under the United States Government listings).

A Social Security representative will guide you through the application process and help you determine whether or not you are eligible for additional state payments, food stamps, or Medicaid. In some cases of extreme need, Social Security can arrange for applicants to receive an immediate advance on their SSI benefits.

HOW TO DEFEND YOUR RIGHT TO SSI BENEFITS

Because the eligibility requirements for SSI benefits are so complicated, mistakes, miscalculations, and misinterpretations of regulations can and do occur when applications are initially processed. If you or a friend or relative is turned down initially, you should immediately take advantage of the appeals process and the sources of assistance described in Chapter 5. In addition, you may find it helpful to contact your local welfare agency (see your telephone directory under your local government listings).

For more information about SSI contact the Social Security Administration:

▶ Pamphlet: *SSI*
Cost: Free
From: Your local Social Security office or

Office of Public Inquiry
Social Security Administration
Department of Health and Human Services
6401 Security Boulevard
Baltimore, MD 21235

— ≡ 7 ≡ —

Your Guide to Medicare and Medicaid

Medicare is a federal health insurance program for people age 65 and older, as well as for certain people under age 65 who have been collecting Social Security disability benefits for at least 24 months. The hospital expenses covered under Medicare are financed by the Social Security taxes paid by you, other workers, and employers. The medical expenses covered under Medicare are financed by the general revenues of the U.S. government and monthly premiums paid by those enrolled.

You are automatically entitled to Medicare coverage if you are receiving or are entitled to receive:

• Social Security benefits
• Railroad retirement benefits
• Federal government pensions

If you haven't earned enough work credits to be eligible for Social Security benefits, you can enroll in Medicare but you have to pay for the coverage out of your own pocket. In 1990, that cost was $175 per month. Eligibility for free Medicare hospital insurance is yet another reason why it is so important that all of your earnings be accurately reported to Social Security.

WHAT COSTS DOES MEDICARE COVER?

Medicare has two parts, Part A and Part B. Part A is free. Part B is optional and, in 1990, carried a charge of $31 per month. This monthly charge is deducted from your Social Security check if you are receiving benefits or billed to you if you are not yet retired. The coverage provided by Medicare includes hospitalization insurance and medical insurance.

Part A: Hospitalization Insurance

Part A covers:

• Up to 90 days per year for a semiprivate room and board, nursing and miscellaneous hospital services, and supplies
• 100 days of skilled nursing care in an acute care institution
• Medically necessary skilled nursing care at home
• Hospice care for the terminally ill
• Blood transfusions

Under Part A, the patient is responsible for paying significant deductibles and coinsurance payments. For example, in 1990, patients paid deductibles of $592 for each hospital stay. Medicare paid the remaining hospital charges for the first 60 days of hospitalization. For days 61 to 90, patients paid a coinsurance charge of $148 per day. Medicare also paid all the costs of the first 20 days of skilled nursing home care but charged a coinsurance payment of $74 per day for days 21 to 100. Skilled nursing care at home, hospice care, and blood transfusions also involved copayments.

Part B: Medical Insurance

Part B covers:

• Physician and surgeon services in or out of hospitals, except for routine physical exams

• Medical services and supplies received on an outpatient basis, such as x-rays, lab tests, ambulance service, and wheelchairs
• Physical therapy and speech therapy, if done under a doctor's supervision

The most important fact to understand about Part B coverage is that all reimbursements are based upon Medicare's *approved fee* for that product or service. For example, Medicare's approved fee for a certain procedure may be $50. If you've satisfied your annual deductible, Medicare will pay 80 percent of this fee, or $40. However, your doctor may actually charge $75 for the procedure, leaving you with a bill for $35. Any medical expenses you pay over the approved fee do not count toward your annual deductible or the yearly out-of-pocket expense limit.

Medicare pays 80 percent of the approved charge for each product or service after you pay an annual $75 deductible. Medicare will pay 100 percent of approved charges after you reach your yearly out-of-pocket expense limit—that is, after your combined expenses of the $75 deductible and the 20 percent coinsurance payments have reached $1,370.

Although Medicare is an extremely valuable program, the combined benefits of Part A and Part B cover only about half the medical costs of the average recipient. In addition to the deductible and coinsurance payments, recipients are responsible for paying the costs of:

• Private duty nursing
• Skilled nursing home care beyond 100 days per year
• Custodial care in a nursing home or at home
• Routine physical exams and immunizations
• Prescription drugs
• Routine foot care
• Dental care
• Eyeglasses or hearing aids
• Care received outside of the United States

Most recipients find it necessary to purchase private "Medigap" insurance to meet these and other additional costs.

HOW TO APPLY FOR MEDICARE

You are eligible for Medicare when you turn 65, even if you are not retired or do not plan to retire at 65. You will definitely want to enroll in both Part A and Part B if you have no health insurance. You will also want to enroll in both parts if you are paying for private health insurance, because the coverage provided by Medicare will dramatically reduce your premiums (see pages 68–70 on how to shop for supplemental "Medigap" insurance).

In addition, many employers that provide health insurance coverage require eligible employees to enroll in both Part A and Part B of Medicare because it reduces the company's expenditures. Even if your company continues to provide full coverage, you should enroll in Part A during your initial enrollment period. Although federal law requires that hospital claims be submitted to your private carrier first, you will have the assurance that this free coverage is already in force when you need it.

Medicare is administered by the Health Care Financing Administration. However, your local Social Security office will answer your questions and will help you apply in writing for the program. When you apply for Medicare Part A, you are automatically enrolled in Part B unless you specifically refuse coverage. In 1990, the monthly premium for Part B coverage was $31.

The regulations on when you can apply for Medicare are stringent and a little complicated. If you don't pay attention to these regulations, you may find yourself without coverage for several months. Explanations of the regulations regarding enrollment periods follow:

Three Enrollment Periods for Medicare

1. Initial Enrollment Period. You become eligible for Medicare either when you turn 65 (whether or not you are retired) or when you have collected Social Security disability benefits for 24 months. You can apply for Medicare for a period of seven months. This initial enrollment period begins on the first day of the third month *before* the month of your 65th birthday (or your 25th month on disability) and ends on the last day of the fourth month *after* the month of your birthday. For example, if you will turn 65 on April 10, you can apply any time from January 1 to July 31.

2. General enrollment period. If you fail to apply during your initial enrollment period, you can only apply for Medicare during the period of January 1 to March 31 of each calendar year.

If you have declined Part B coverage when you enroll for Part A, you must wait until the next general enrollment period to sign up if your circumstances change.

3. Special enrollment period. There is a special seven-month enrollment period for people who work past age 65 and are covered under an employer health plan. This period begins on the first day of the first month in which the employee is no longer covered by an employer health plan. For example, if you retire from a job at age 67 on March 15, you can apply for Medicare any time from March 1 to September 30.

If you apply during any enrollment period, your coverage begins on the date of application.

The Federal Consolidated Omnibus Budget Reconciliation Act of 1985 (COBRA) requires most employers with group health insurance plans to continue coverage of retired and unemployed former employees and their dependents for a minimum of 18 months. The employer may charge the former employee, but that charge cannot exceed the normal group rate plus a 2 percent service charge. Dependents may be entitled to coverage after the death of or divorce from a former employee. To find out more, call or write for the following booklets:

▶ Booklet: *Consumer Notes: Group Health Insurance Continuation*
Cost: Free
From: Health Insurance Association of America
(800) 423-8000

▶ Booklet: *Group Health Insurance Continuation*
Cost: Free (with self-addressed stamped envelope)
From: Older Women's League
730 Eleventh Street NW
Washington, DC 20001
(202) 783-6686

If you feel that you have been unfairly denied the right to continue your health insurance coverage, you should contact the Department of Labor:

▶ Resource: Department of Labor
Division of Technical Assistance
Room North 5658
200 Constitution Avenue NW
Washington, DC 20210
(202) 523-8784

HOW TO REDUCE YOUR EXPENDITURES UNDER MEDICARE

There are several ways that you can reduce your expenditures under Medicare.

1. Keep any group insurance offered by your employer as part of your on-the-job or retirement benefits. Private health insurance tends to be more inclusive than Medicare, so you could decline enrollment for Part B and save the expense of that premium—as long as your employer does not require you to enroll in Part B.

Note: If you have a group insurance policy, federal law requires that you submit bills (claims) to your group insurance carrier before submitting them to Medicare.

2. Find a physician who accepts *assignment*. *Assignment* means that the physician or clinic agrees to charge only the Medicare-approved fees and that Medicare will be billed directly for the 80 percent reimbursement. The assignment system saves you the considerable trouble of filing claims, as well as significantly reducing your initial out-of-pocket expenses.

Unfortunately, many physicians don't accept assignment at all and others accept assignment for only some procedures. You can obtain the names of physicians who accept assignment in your area by consulting the *MediPard Directory*:

▶ Directory: *The MediPard Directory*
   Contains: A list of health care providers in your area
       that accept assignment
   Contact: Your local Social Security office (see your
       telephone directory under the United States
       Government listings)
   Your local area Agency on Aging (see listings on
       pages 44–45)
   Your local public library

---

3. Find a Health Maintenance Organization (HMO) that has signed a contract with the federal government to bill only approved fees. Health Maintenance Organizations are organizations that provide complete medical care in return for a fixed monthly fee. Of special interest to people age 65 and over are HMOs which have signed contracts with the federal government to provide services to Medicare recipients. The HMO will charge you an additional monthly fee that covers your deductibles and coinsurance charges. This arrangement eliminates paperwork and allows budgeting for a fixed monthly medical expense.

To locate HMOs in your area, you should look in the Yellow Pages of your telephone directory under "Health Maintenance Organizations" or contact the national trade association of HMOs:

▶ Organization: Group Health Association of America
1129 20th Street NW, Suite 600
Washington, DC 20036
(202) 778-3200

The AARP will consult a directory to see if there is an HMO near you, if you write:

▶ Organization: Health Advocacy Services
AARP
1909 K Street NW
Washington, DC 20049

For more detailed information on evaluating HMOs, you should send for these booklets:

▶ Booklets: *More Health for Your Dollar: An Older Person's Guide to HMOs*
Choosing an HMO: An Evaluation Checklist
Cost: Free
From: AARP Fulfillment
1909 K Street NW
Washington, DC 20049

▶ Pamphlet: *Medicare and Prepayment Plans*
Cost: Free

From: U.S. Department of Health and Human Services
       Health Care Financing Administration
       East High Rise Building
       6325 Security Boulevard
       Baltimore, MD 21207

HOW TO DEFEND YOUR RIGHTS
UNDER MEDICARE

As the cost of health care in this country continues to soar, Medicare recipients can run into a number of problems that may prevent them from receiving the full benefits to which they are entitled. Among the major problems:

- Physicians and hospitals bill for unnecessary or unauthorized services, procedures, tests, and supplies not covered by Medicare.
- Physicians and hospitals fill out forms improperly or fail to submit forms.
- Increasing pressure to hold down expenditures causes Medicare administrators to increasingly deny benefits rather than give the Medicare recipient the benefit of the doubt.

Because your health is involved and because the costs of serious illness or disability can be huge, correcting problems and challenging administrative decisions on Medicare may be more important to your well-being than challenging rulings on Social Security benefits. That's why you should take the time to become thoroughly familiar with your legal rights, the appeals procedure, and the resources that can help you fight for your rights.

How to Defend Your Rights Under Part A

Part A benefits are paid by the Social Security Trust Fund. However, the Social Security Administration hires private insurance companies called *intermediaries* to process Part A claims and handle first-level appeals. Your Medicare Part A intermediary must have a toll-free telephone number that you can call to:

• Check on the status of a claim or appeal.
• Ask for clarification of a statement.
• Obtain duplicate copies of claims.

This toll-free number is listed in *Your Medicare Handbook* that you receive when you enroll in the program. It is also available by calling your local Social Security office.

Some claims under Part A are referred to another company known as a *Peer Review Organization (PRO)*, which is hired by the government to monitor the quality of care given to the recipients and to determine if the care was necessary in complicated cases. Some claims are chosen at random for review, while others are referred because of the size of the claim or the complexity of the medical care involved. The telephone number of your PRO is available from your local Social Security office.

If you disagree with the handling of a claim by either the intermediary or the PRO under Part A, you can take the following steps:

Step 1: Ask for Reconsideration

If your claim is denied or not paid in full, you will receive an Explanation of Medicare Benefits form that explains the reason. You can give this to your physician, hospital, or other medical provider and ask them for additional information that addresses this reason. For example, your physician may have to provide detailed justification for medical tests in order to prove they were necessary.

Once you have the additional information, you can ask for a reconsideration by filling out Form SSA-2649. *You must file within 60 days of the initial determination.* Another decision will be made by the intermediary or the PRO based on the new evidence and any additional medical records you submit.

Step 2: Hearing Before an Administrative Judge

If your reconsideration is unfavorable and the amount in question is more than $100 ($200 if the decision was made by the PRO), you can ask for a hearing before an administrative law judge by filing Form HA-501.1 at your local Social Security office. A hearing will be scheduled at a site no more than 75 miles from your home. At this informal hearing, you can:

• Present new evidence.
• Be represented by counsel.
• Call and question witnesses.

Step 3: A Review by the Appeals Council

If your appeal is denied after the hearing, you can request a review by the SSA's three-person Appeals Council. *You must request the review within 60 days of receiving a decision from your hearing.* You can request the review by filing Form HA-520 at your local Social Security office.

Step 4: Request a Federal Court Hearing

If your claim is for a sum greater than $1,000 ($2,000 for PRO decisions), you can hire an attorney and file a court complaint with a federal district court. *You must file within 60 days of a decision by the Appeals Council.*

How to Defend Your Rights Under Part B

Because you go to the doctor more often than you enter a hospital, many more claims are submitted for you under Part

B than Part A. Since many doctors don't accept assignment for many procedures, the Medicare-approved payment is often less than the amount you are billed for, with the difference coming out of your pocket. As a result, many experts, including AARP, urge Medicare recipients to exercise their right to appeal when the amount paid is significantly less than the amount billed. For example, you may have been billed $150 for an office visit and Medicare only approved $100. Studies have shown that only a small percentage of Part B claims decisions are appealed, but that *more than half of these appeals are successful.*

Part B benefits are paid by premiums you pay and by contributions from the U.S. Treasury. The federal government hires private insurance companies, known as *carriers*, to process claims and handle appeals. Your Medicare Part B carrier has a toll-free telephone number that you can call to:

• Check on the status of a claim or appeal.
• Ask for clarification of a statement.
• Obtain duplicate copies of claims.

This toll-free number is listed in *Your Medicare Handbook* that you receive when you enroll in the program. It is also available by calling your local Social Security office.

If you disagree with a decision made by your carrier, you have the right to appeal through the following steps:

Step 1: Request a Review

You can request a review of an initial determination by submitting Form HCFA-1964 to your carrier. *You must do so within six months of receiving your Explanation of Medicare Benefits form.* You can send any additional information from your doctor with this form. However, many reviewers will increase the Medicare payment without any additional information.

Step 2: Request a Hearing

If your review is unfavorable, you can request a hearing on your appeal by filing Form HCFA-1965 for claims of $100 to $499 or Form HCFA-501.1 for claims of $500 or more. *You must file your request within six months of receiving the review decision.* The carrier will conduct telephone interviews or hold an informal in-person hearing.

Step 3: Request a Hearing Before an Administrative Law Judge

If a claim of $500 or more is still in dispute after the hearing by the carrier, you may contact your local Social Security office to request a hearing by an administrative law judge. *You must request the hearing within 60 days of the decision based on the carrier's hearing.*

Step 4: Request a Review by the Appeals Council

You have the right to request a review by the Appeals Council within 60 days of the decision by the administrative law judge. You can request a review by contacting your local Social Security office.

Step 5: Request a Federal Court Hearing

If your claim is for $1,000 or more, you can hire an attorney to request a hearing from a federal district court. *You must request the hearing within 60 days of the decision by the Appeals Council.*

How to Obtain Help in Exercising Your Right to a Medicare Appeal

The AARP advises that talking to someone who really knows about the Medicare system is one of the best ways to ensure you get all of the Medicare benefits you're entitled to receive. Two major programs can put you in touch with the expert help you will need:

▶ Program: Medicare Advocacy
   Services: Federal law requires every area's Agency on Aging to use a portion of their funding for legal assistance to people age 60 and over, including assistance and counseling for people on Medicare.
   For information: Call your local area Agency on Aging. To get the number, call your state Agency on Aging (see listings on pages 44–45).

▶ Program: Medicare/Medicaid Assistance Program
   Services: The AARP has trained volunteers to help Medicare recipients with claims and appeals in more than 32 states. For a list of programs in or near your state, write:
   Medicare/Medicaid Assistance Project
   AARP
   1909 K Street NW
   Washington, DC 20049

You can also help yourself by learning as much about Medicare as you can. Among the sources of information are:

▶ Booklets: *Medicare: What It Covers, What It Doesn't (D13133)*
   Knowing Your Rights: Medicare's Prospective Payment System (D12330)
   Cost: Free
   From: AARP Fulfillment
       1909 K Street NW
       Washington, DC 20049

▶ Book: *Your Real Medicare Handbook*
   Cost: $8.00
   Contains: Detailed, easy-to-understand explanation of

Medicare programs, forms, and appeal procedures
From: Center for Public Representation
121 South Pinckney Street
Madison, WI 53703

▶ Organization: Legal Counsel for the Elderly
Services: A national support center to improve the
quality of legal services to older Americans.
Publications: *Self-Help Handbook: Medicare* ($6.95
plus $2.00 postage)
Medicare series, four practical guides that help
resolve Medicare problems:
Eligibility Book ($5.95 plus $1.00 postage)
General Problems Book ($5.95 plus $1.00
postage)
*Hospital, Hospice, and Nursing Home Care
Book*($5.95 plus $1.00 postage)
Doctor Services ($5.95 plus $1.00 postage)
All four $19.95 plus $2.50 postage
From: LCE, Inc.
PO Box 96474
Washington, DC 20090

Warning: Beware of Medicare Consultants

Because Medicare is so complex, a large number of small
businesses offer to process Medicare claims and pursue appeals in return for a fee. This field has attracted a significant
number of con artists who make elaborate promises and
charge exorbitant fees.

To avoid fraud:

• Beware of people who promise you very large settlements to
claims rejected by Medicare.
• Before you pay, check out the company by calling your local
Better Business Bureau or your state or local consumer
protection agency.

HOW TO PURCHASE PRIVATE "MEDIGAP" INSURANCE

In the last decade, many companies have eliminated or reduced health care coverage for retirees. Therefore, a majority of Americans ages 65 and over need to purchase supplemental "Medigap" policies that fill some or all of the "gaps" in Medicare coverage.

This need has produced hundreds of different policies, many of which are offered to consumers through television advertising, direct mail, and even telephone solicitation. However, the quality and costs of these policies vary widely. The worst of these policies are a waste of money because they virtually duplicate Medicare coverage; the best provide nearly complete coverage against catastrophic illness.

The first step in purchasing a "Medigap" policy is to obtain a benchmark quotation from an insurance program that has been highly rated by consumer advocates. That program is:

▶ Program: AARP Group Health Insurance Program
   Services: Medicare supplement plan for AARP
      members
   For information: AARP Group Health Insurance
                    Program
                    PO Box 7000
                    Allentown, PA 18175
                    (800) 523-5800 (Except PA)
                    (800) 492-2024 (in PA)

The second step is to take advantage of publications and information resources that will help you compare and evaluate individual policies. Because Medicare itself is complicated, this process can be more difficult than purchasing other forms of insurance, such as life or automobile insurance. Among these resources are:

▶ Organization: Health Care Financing Administration
Services: Operates toll-free hotline to answer questions
   about Medicare.
Publication: *Guide To Health Insurance for People
   with Medicare*
Cost: Free
Contact: Department of Health and Human Services
         Health Care Financing Administration
         6325 Security Boulevard
         Baltimore, MD 21207
         (800) 888-1998

▶ Booklets: *Information on Medicare and Health
            Insurance for Older People
   The Prudent Patient*
Cost: Free
From: AARP Fulfillment
      1909 K Street NW
      Washington, DC 20049

▶ Booklets: *Health Care Finances: A Guide for Adult
            Children and Their Parents
   The Consumer's Guide to Medicare Supplement
   Insurance*
Cost: Free
From: Health Insurance Association of America
      1001 Pennsylvania Avenue NW
      Washington, DC 20004
      (800) 423-8000

▶ Fact Sheets: *Factsheets on Medicare and Health Care*
Cost: Free
From: National Consumers League
      815 15th Street NW, Suite 516
      Washington, DC 20005

▶ Organization: Your state insurance department
Services: Many state insurance departments have
   publications explaining Medicare and supplementary
   health insurance programs. This department may

also provide information on the level of complaints
registered against specific insurance companies.
For information: See your telephone directory under
your state government listings.

YOUR GUIDE TO MEDICAID

Medicaid is a joint federal/state program that supplements
Medicare by providing comprehensive health care benefits for
people ages 65 and older and disabled individuals who have
very low incomes and assets. Generally, people who meet the
guidelines for receiving Supplementary Social Security benefits (see Chapter 6) should contact their local Social Security
offices or their local area's Agency on Aging (see the listing
on pages 44–45) to see if they are also eligible for Medicaid.
Because Medicaid is a joint federal/state program, however,
the laws governing eligibility do vary from state to state.

If you should be eligible for Medicaid, the additional benefits would make the purchase of private Medigap insurance
unnecessary.

PART II:

PROTECT YOUR PENSION RIGHTS AND BENEFITS

═ 8 ═

Understanding Your Company Pension Plan

WHAT IS A PENSION?

A pension is any plan, fund, or program established by an employer, group of employers, or union which provides retirement income to employees or results in a deferral of income by employees until they leave the job or later. An employer is under no legal obligation to provide a pension plan. But in fact, in 1990, 76.1 million Americans (46 percent of American workers) were covered by 870,000 pension plans. If you are one of them, you probably count on pension benefits as a crucial part of your retirement income.

Unfortunately, Congressional studies project that one-third of those 76.1 million workers will never get one dime from the pension plan under which they are currently working. Millions of other workers will get only part of the money they counted on. And surviving spouses of retired pension recipients fare the worst—only 3 percent of older American women are collecting monthly checks from the deceased husband's pensions.

Over the last two decades, fraud and abuses of the pension system by employers and unions has led Congress to enact a series of laws designed to regulate some aspects of the operation of a pension fund. However, as of late 1990, the U.S.

Department of Labor had 300 auditors who could examine only 1 percent of the nation's 870,000 pension plans each year.

This effort is becoming more and more inadequate as an increasing number of corporations raid pension funds and eliminate expensive benefits to pay for acquisitions, buy back stock, or fend off takeover attempts. Yet corporate managements encounter few protests from employees, because pension plans are among the least understood of all employee benefits.

The enormous costs incurred when inadequate government supervision resulted in the recent savings and loan scandal has led many Congressional leaders to pay even more attention to a pension situation that the inspector general of the Department of Labor has called "ripe for scandal." However, until new laws are passed, your primary protection is to:

• Fully understand your pension program.
• Monitor how your pension is administered.
• Defend your pension rights.

Your Pension Plan Is Part of Your Overall Compensation

Although the federal government oversees the fairness and honesty of your pension fund, there are no rules or regulations about how much an employer should contribute, how pension benefits are calculated, or how much each employee should receive when he or she retires. Two employees earning the same base salary for the same period of time for two different employers could draw monthly pension checks hundreds of dollars apart when they retire.

The best time to obtain information about a pension plan is before you accept a job. At that time, you must realize that your employer's contribution to your pension is part of your total employee wage and benefit package. A company that offers significantly more money in salary and bonuses may offer either no pension plan or much more modest benefits. If current income is more important to you, or if you are in a field where you change jobs frequently, you may even ignore company pension benefits entirely and concentrate on saving for your retirement on your own through Individual Retirement Accounts (IRAs).

If you have worked for a company for a significant period of time and plan to make a career with that company, you no longer have the option of choosing pension plans offered by other companies. But obtaining information about your plan early in your career is important in planning your financial future, in insuring that you get all the benefits to which you are entitled, and in defending yourself against any efforts to modify or eliminate your pension plan.

YOUR PLAN ADMINISTRATION

Federal law requires that all employees ages 21 and over must become participants in the plan after two years of employment. The majority of plans require only one year of employment before you become eligible. If you are an older worker, you should consider this period of eligibility before you take a job. Federal law also states that no employee can be excluded from a plan or dropped from a plan because of age, sex, race, marital status, or disability.

Every pension plan must be supervised by a plan administrator. Your company personnel office must provide you with the name, mailing address, and telephone number of the plan administrator. Federal law requires that within 90 days after you become eligible for your pension plan, you must receive from the plan administrator a *summary plan description*, a booklet or similar document that in easy-to-understand language explains:

- How the plan operates
- When you're eligible to receive a pension
- How to calculate your benefits
- How to file a claim

The plan administrator is also obligated by federal law to

provide you with *survivor coverage data*, which informs you of the plan's survivor coverage and how it affects you and your spouse.

Although federal law doesn't require an employer to provide a summary plan description to prospective employers or employees not yet eligible to participate, many companies will. If a prospective or present employer will not voluntarily give you this information, you can obtain a copy of the summary plan description for your plan and the latest pension fund annual report from:

▶ Organization: Department of Labor
   Public Disclosure Room
   Room N-5707
   200 Constitution Avenue NW
   Washington, DC 20210
   (202) 523-8771
   Fee: $.10 per page for copies

UNDERSTANDING YOUR SUMMARY PLAN DESCRIPTION

Your summary plan description will include information about how your type of plan operates, when you will be eligible to receive benefits, how your benefits are calculated, and how to file a claim.

How Your Plan Operates

There are two basic types of pension plans:

- *Defined benefit plans* promise a specified monthly benefit upon retirement computed on a formula based on years of service and annual income. These plans are normally funded entirely by employer contributions.

- *Defined contribution plans* promise only that your employer make a specific contribution to your retirement account each year. This contribution may be a specific amount of money or, under a profit sharing plan, a specific percentage of profits. In many cases, employees can make an additional tax-deductible contribution to the pension fund from their wages and salaries. The pension benefit paid at retirement depends on how successfully the money in an individual's account was invested.

Defined Benefit Plans

About 70 percent of all workers covered by pensions have defined benefit plans. The advantages of defined benefit plans are:

- They are financed from employer contributions.
- The amount of the benefits is clearly stated.
- At least part of the benefits of most defined benefit plans are guaranteed by the U.S. government in case the company defaults.

The disadvantages of defined benefit plans are:

- Benefits are very modest, normally averaging 1.5 percent of your annual salary for each year of service. That means a worker earning $20,000 after 10 years would receive $250 per month.
- Your pension may be paid as a fixed monthly sum that is steadily eroded over the years by inflation. At an inflation rate of 5 percent, the purchasing power of your benefits would be cut in half in 14 years.
- An increasing number of companies are taking for their own use the excess investment income generated by these pension funds instead of using it to increase benefits.

- You receive nothing from the pension fund if you leave your job before your right to receive a pension becomes permanent, or *vested*.

Defined Contribution Plans

Defined contribution plans are becoming increasingly popular, because they free employers from the legal obligation to pay fixed benefits. These plans can take many forms, the most common of which are profit sharing plans and 401(k) plans. The advantages of defined contribution plans are:

- Total annual contributions can be as high as 25 percent of your salary, to a maximum of $30,000.
- Contributions out of your salary are tax-deductible up to $7,000 per year.
- Employees benefit from all investment income, which means benefits can be much larger than fixed benefits from a defined benefit plan.
- In some cases, employees can choose how their pension funds are invested.
- At retirement, the amount in the pension fund can be taken as a lump sum as well as converted to an annuity. That allows you to invest the money to compensate for inflation.
- The funds you have contributed will be given you in a lump sum at any time, should you leave the company.

The disadvantages of defined contribution plans are:

- These funds are not federally guaranteed.
- An employee can suffer from poor returns on investment of contributions.
- Profit sharing contributions may drop or stop if the company has financial problems.
- Employer contributions may be reduced or eliminated without consulting the employee.
- An employee can withdraw or borrow against pension contributions only in case of serious emergencies.

- Retiring employees who receive a lump-sum pension settlement are often tempted to spend the money rather than reinvest it for income.

When You Are Eligible to Receive a Pension

This part of your summary plan description will provide the following important information:

- When you are eligible to participate in the pension plan. We discussed this earlier in this chapter on page 75
- When your right to receive a pension will become permanent, or vested
- When you are eligible to be drawing pension benefits

Federal law requires that your right to receive pension benefits becomes vested after a certain period of employment. After your rights are vested, you will receive the benefit you have earned even if you leave your job. The period of time required by law depends on when your pension plan was started and how long you have been a member of that plan. After studies showed that nearly one-third of all employees currently enrolled in pension plans will never collect a dime in pension benefits because they don't work for the company long enough, a new federal law was passed in 1989 stipulating that new pension plans allow an employee to become fully vested after five years of employment. Many new plans provide for partial vesting after as little as one year of employment, greatly increasing an employee's chances of eventually collecting pension benefits.

Under many defined contribution plans, you are entitled to receive at least the proceeds of your contributions in a lump sum when you leave your job. You can then invest this sum in your new company's defined contribution plan or an Individual Retirement Account (IRA) without incurring taxes or penalties. This feature has made defined contribution plans increasingly popular with employees.

Most pension plans define both an early retirement date and a normal retirement date. If you retire early, your monthly benefit is normally much lower than if you retire at the normal retirement date.

How Your Benefits Are Calculated

If you are in a defined benefit plan, your benefits are determined by a unique formula that relates your monthly check at the time of retirement to past employment and wages, your age, your years of service, and the effects of inflation. The result may favor employees who meet certain types of criteria. For example, a plan may give proportionately greater benefits for long-term service, for management rather than blue-collar employees, or to employees with the highest wages at the time of retirement. It is especially important that you consider any bias in the pension plan before you take a job.

One final and extremely important factor that can affect your monthly benefits is any provision to reduce an individual's defined benefits by a portion of the Social Security benefits he or she receives. This practice is especially damaging to lower-income workers whose pension benefits may only be $200 to $300 a month to begin with. If you are counting on pension income to provide a substantial portion of your support after retirement, you should think very carefully about accepting a job with a pension plan that reduces its benefits based on your Social Security benefits.

Pension benefits from a defined contribution plan are much more difficult to determine in advance because they depend on the exact amount of the contribution and the performance of your pension fund's investments. An increasing number of these plans allow the employee to make some decisions about how the money will be invested. For example, an employee may be allowed to choose between long-term-growth investments such as common stocks, income-producing investments such as bonds, or very safe but conservative investments such as U.S. Treasury bonds and money market mutual funds.

How to File a Claim

Your employer will normally guide you through this process if you retire while still an employee. However, your spouse and dependents should know where you keep information on filing a claim in the event of your death or disability.

If you are entitled to pension payments under a defined benefit plan as an ex-employee, federal law requires that you be given information on how to apply for those benefits when you leave the company. It is your obligation, however, to keep your former employer informed of any address changes so that you can be notified of changes in the pension plan or in the procedures for applying for benefits.

UNDERSTANDING YOUR SURVIVOR COVERAGE DATA

According to the chairman of the House Subcommittee on Retirement Income and Employment, only 3 percent of American women were receiving any kind of surviving spouse pension benefits in 1990. In 1984, Congress attempted to deal with this problem by requiring that pension plans enacted after that date must offer a benefit that includes payment to a spouse after the death of the pensioner. However, the monthly check received by an employee who retires under a joint survivor plan can be as little as half the amount of the benefit paid to a retiring employee whose benefits will end at his or her death.

As a result, many pension plan participants waive their right to a joint survivor benefit in order to increase the monthly check they will receive when they retire. Beginning in 1985, however, federal law stipulated that *both* the employee and the spouse must sign the waiver if they choose not to claim joint survivor benefits. This new regulation may prevent the shock many spouses experience if pension checks suddenly end at the death of a pension recipient.

For more information on your rights as a surviving or divorced spouse, see Chapter 11.

WHAT HAPPENS WHEN YOUR PLAN IS CHANGED

If your employer makes any changes in information that is required to be in the summary plan description, your plan administrator must send you a copy of those changes within 210 days of the end of the year in which the changes take place. In addition, you must receive a brand new summary plan description every five years if there have been any amendments to the plan, or every 10 years if there have been no amendments to the plan.

FOR MORE INFORMATION

The subject of pensions is very complicated. You can obtain more valuable information about pension plans from the following booklets:

▶ Booklets: *What You Should Know About the Pension Law*
Often-Asked Questions About Employee Retirement Benefits
Cost: Free
From: Office of Public Affairs
Pension and Welfare Benefits Administration
U.S. Department of Labor
200 Constitution Avenue NW
Washington, DC 20210

▶ Booklet: *Your Pension: Things You Should Know About Your Pension Plan*
Cost: Free

From: Pension Benefit Guaranty Corporation
2020 K Street NW
Washington, DC 20006

▶ Booklet: *A Guide to Understanding Your Pension Plan*
Cost: $3.50
From: The Pension Rights Center
918 16th Street NW Suite 704
Washington, DC 20006

$$\equiv 9 \equiv$$

How to Obtain an Estimate of Your Pension Earnings and Benefits

HOW TO OBTAIN INFORMATION ABOUT YOUR PERSONAL PENSION ACCOUNT

A Congressional study revealed that only one in sixteen workers who participated in a pension plan could accurately estimate the pension benefits they were likely to receive when they retired. An accurate estimate is crucial information in retirement planning, a process that should begin decades before you retire. Many retirees face "pension shock," the discovery that their benefits will be inadequate to meet their expenses at a time when it is too late to start any personal retirement savings plan.

How can you tell what pension benefits you are likely to receive? Federal law requires that, upon written request, your plan administrator must provide you with a statement of:

• The total benefits that you have earned to date
• The amount of these benefits which are vested
• The date upon which all of your benefits will be vested

A form letter, which can be sent to your plan administrator, follows. Federal law allows you to request this personal information once every 12 months.

TO: Plan Administrator

_____

_____

_____

_____

FROM: _____

_____

_____

_____

I formally request that you provide me with:

- A statement of my total accrued pension benefits, the amount of those benefits which is vested, and the date on which all of these benfits have or will become vested
- A copy of the latest summary plan description
- A copy of the latest annual report
- Information on the survivor coverage in my pension plan

Thank you for your assistance.

Sincerely,

_____

WHAT TO DO WHEN YOU RECEIVE YOUR PERSONAL BENEFITS STATEMENT

If you submit a letter based upon the preceding form letter, you will receive two additional documents with your personal benefits statement, both of which you are entitled to receive under federal law:

• The latest updated summary plan description
• The latest annual report for the pension fund

You should sit down with all three documents. How you check the documents depends on whether you have a defined benefit plan or a defined contribution plan.

Defined Benefit Plans

Defined benefit plans provide a predetermined benefit based on your *years of service* under the pension plan and your income during those years. Therefore, it is extremely important that you verify:

1. The years of service with which you have been credited. For pension purposes, your years of service are limited to the years in which you were a participant in the pension program. If your company requires two years of employment before you become eligible, your years of service are computed from the beginning of your third year with the company.

Current federal law requires that your pension plan give you credit for one year of service for each calendar year (after you become eligible) in which you were paid for 1,000 hours, including sick pay, vacation pay, disability, jury duty, and military leave. You can accumulate 1,000 hours by averaging just 20 hours a week over a 50-week work year.

Federal law also requires that employers credit you with years of service both before and after *breaks of service*, or interruptions in your employment. Among the most common reasons why people interrupt their employment are military service, parental leave, medical disability, or returning to school. A break in service is normally defined as any year in which you were paid for less than 500 hours. Your employer is generally required to credit you for all years worked if the number of years you took off from work is equal to or less than the number of years' service you had earned before you interrupted your employment. For example, if you were credited for five years of service before you took two years off to return to graduate school, you would receive credit for those five years. However, if you had earned only one year of service before taking two years off, your employer would not be required to credit you with that year when you returned to work.

Some pension plans, particularly those established before 1976 or those of companies with less than 25 employees, may legally apply more stringent rules for crediting years of service or dealing with breaks in service. On the other hand, many companies have more lenient policies. Your summary plan description should have an explanation of the requirements for your plan. If you don't understand these requirements or you believe you have not been credited with the years of service you have earned, you should make an appointment with the plan administrator.

2. Verify the percentage of your benefits which are vested and the date upon which they will become fully vested. Depending on when your pension plan started, federal law mandates full vesting sometime between five and fifteen years. Partial vesting can begin between one and ten years of service. Federal law also requires that you become fully vested when you reach full retirement age, even if you have not earned the required years of service.

The vesting provisions of your pension plan are included in your summary plan description. If you don't understand them or disagree about the percentage of vesting you have acquired, you should make an appointment with the plan administrator.

3. Estimate your benefits. Your personal benefit statement may include an estimate of the benefits you would receive at retirement. If not, you can consult your summary plan description to find out how benefits are determined.

Most defined benefit plans set forth a formula which determines your monthly benefits. Some are very simple, such as $10 per month for every year of service you have earned. If you will have been with the company 23 years at retirement age, you would receive a pension of $230 per month.

Many pension plans provide for a specific percentage of your average monthly salary for each year of service. For example, your plan may provide for a monthly payment of 1.5 percent of your average monthly wages of $2,000 for each year of service. If you retire after 23 years, your monthly check would be:

$$1.5\% \times \$2,000 \times 23 = \$690 \text{ per month}$$

Still other plans use more complicated formulas, including those that pay proportionately greater benefits to workers who have been with the company longer at retirement age.

If you are not confident that you are accurately estimating your pension benefits based on the years of service you have earned and the annual wages you have been paid, you should seek the assistance of your plan administrator.

Defined Contribution Plans

Defined contribution plans require that the employer make a specified contribution to your retirement account for each year of service. Many plans allow you to contribute to your retirement account from your wages or salary. Therefore, it is extremely important that you verify:

1. Your years of service. In a defined contribution plan, your employer's obligation is only to make a contribution for each year of service. The federal laws defining what constitutes a year of service are the same for defined contribution plans as for defined benefit plans (see page 86). It is extremely important that you contact your plan administrator if you do not believe you have received enough credit.

2. The amount of your benefits that are vested and the date on which they will become fully vested. *All contributions you make to your pension plan are always fully and immediately vested.* Federal laws governing the vesting of your rights to funds contributed by your employer, however, are the same for both defined benefit and defined contribution plans. Your summary plan description explains the vesting requirements for your pension plan. If you have any questions or problems, contact your plan administrator immediately.

3. The amount of contributions made by your employer and by you. Every participant in a defined contribution plan has an individual pension account. Your personal benefit statement should list the contributions from you and your employer for every year of service.

Errors in these records do occur, often because of clerical errors. You can check your contributions by comparing your benefit statement to your annual tax returns. Verifying the accuracy of your employer's contributions may be more difficult, especially if these contributions are based on profit sharing or a complex formula. This formula is explained in your summary plan description. If you believe that your employer's contributions are too low for one or more years, you should ask your plan administrator to provide you with the calculations on which those contributions were based.

4. The manner in which your pension funds are invested. Some defined contribution plans allow a participant to decide how some or all of his or her pension funds are invested by providing a choice between a small portfolio of mutual funds with investment objectives ranging from aggressive growth to conservative current income. If you are allowed to make a choice, you should annually verify that your funds have in fact been invested as you directed by requesting this information from your plan administrator.

5. Estimate your retirement benefits. This estimate is difficult to compute accurately for two reasons:

1. You may not know exactly how much you and your employer will contribute every year until retirement.
2. The rate of return on your investment fund will vary from year to year.

Despite the difficulty, you do need a rough approximation of the income you can expect in order to plan for retirement. You can obtain that approximation by following this procedure:

- Assume a moderately conservative 8 percent annual return on the investment of the funds in your pension account.
- Compute the value of the money you *currently* have in your account using the following table.

At 8 percent interest compounded annually, $1,000 will grow to:

5 years	$1,539
10 years	$2,159
15 years	$3,172
20 years	$4,661
25 years	$6,848
30 years	$10,063

For example, if you have $19,000 in your account and you will retire in 20 years, your current balance will be worth:

$$19 \times \$4,661 = \$88,559$$

- Estimate the average annual contribution you and your employer will make to your pension fund every year until you retire. For example, the contribution may total $2,000 per year for 20 years.

At 8 percent interest compounded annually, $1,000 invested annually will grow to:

5 years	$5,870
10 years	$14,490
15 years	$27,150
20 years	$47,760
25 years	$73,100
30 years	$113,290

In 20 years, investing $2,000 per year will yield:

$$2 \times \$47,760 = \$91,520$$

• The total in your retirement account will be:

$$\$88,559 \times \$91,520 = \$180,079$$

Invested at 8 percent, this lump sum will bring you a monthly return of $1,200.53.

HOW TO USE THE ESTIMATE OF YOUR PENSION BENEFITS

After obtaining estimates of your Social Security and pension benefits, you can move on to the extremely important stage of financial planning for your retirement. This process involves three steps:

Step 1: Determine your annual financial needs during your retirement years.

If you are close to retirement, you will probably be able to calculate your annual costs for housing, health care, transportation, food, insurance, travel, and other individual items in your budget.

If you are still years away, experts suggest that you plan on spending 70 percent to 80 percent of your current expenses—adjusted for inflation.

Here's how to make that calculation. If you currently require $25,000 per year to meet your expenses, your retirement expenses in current dollars would be $17,000 to $20,000 per year. To adjust that figure for an average annual inflation rate of 4 percent, consult the table below for the approximate number of years until your retirement:

Year	Multiplier
5	1.22
10	1.48
15	1.80
20	2.19
25	2.67
30	3.24

Multiply your retirement expenses in current dollars by the figure under the Multiplier column. For example, if you will retire in 10 years, your approximate expenses would be:

$$\$17,000 \times 1.48 = \$25,160$$

Because it is extremely difficult to predict accurately annual average inflation and increases in expenses over decades, you should recalculate your projected expenses every three to five years to see if you need to readjust your retirement savings program.

Step 2: Total the income you can reasonably expect to receive.

This income includes:

• Your estimated Social Security benefits
• Your estimated pension benefits

• Income from any other investments (stocks, bonds, real estate) that you currently own

Step 3: Compare your projected income with your expenditures.

For example, the income for you and your spouse may be:

Social Security	$1,000 per month
Pension	$300 per month
Other	$100 per month
Total	$1,400 per month

Your projected expenses may be $20,000 per year, or $1660 per month.

Step 4: Develop a savings plan to insure the additional income.

For example, investing $1,000 per year in an Individual Retirement Account (IRA) at an annual rate of 8 percent over 20 years will give you a nest egg that will produce $300 per month in income.

ADDITIONAL RESOURCES

There are a number of excellent publications that will guide you step-by-step through the extremely important task of financial planning for your retirement. They include:

▶ Workbook: *Think of Your Future: Preretirement Planning Workbook*
   Cost: $24.95 (AARP member price $18.25) plus $1.75 postage

Contains: 303 pages in three-ring binder. Prepared by
AARP. Includes many worksheets, a list of resources,
and detailed information on setting and meeting
financial goals. Very comprehensive.
From: AARP Books/Scott, Foresman and Co.
    1865 Miner Street
    Des Plaines, IL 60016

▶ Book: *Over 50: The Resource Book for the Second
Half of Your Life*, by Tom and Nancy Biracree
Cost: $14.95
Contains: Comprehensive advice and information on
finances, health care, recreation, housing,
employment, taxes, and every other area of life
involved in retirement planning
From: Harper/Collins

▶ Booklet: *Planning Your Retirement* (D12322)
Cost: Free
Contains: A 20-page overview of retirement planning,
including financial planning
From: AARP Fulfillment
    1909 K Street NW
    Washington, DC 20049

▶ Book: *Looking Ahead: How to Plan Your Successful
Retirement*
Cost: $9.95 ($6.95 AARP member) plus $1.75 postage
Contains: A 92-page guide to retirement planning,
which expands upon the information in the booklet
above.
From: AARP Books/Scott, Foresman and Co.
    1865 Miner Street
    Des Plaines, IL 60016

▶ Workbook: *Looking Ahead to Your Financial Future*
Cost: $9.95
Contains: An excellent overview of financial planning,
with easy-to-use retirement planning worksheets

From: PREP Project
      Long Island University
      Southhampton Campus
      Southhampton, NY 11968

▶ Book: *The Complete Retirement Planning Book*, by
  Peter A. Dickinson
  Cost: $10.95
  Contains: A broad-based guide to retirement planning.
  The section on projecting retirement expenses and
  income includes particularly useful information on
  calculating the effects of inflation.
  From: E. P. Dutton

IF YOU NEED ASSISTANCE IN FINANCIAL PLANNING FOR YOUR RETIREMENT

If you don't feel confident in planning for your retirement
yourself, you may want to seek the help of a financial
planner, an individual who has been trained to design short-
term or long-term investment goals for clients, including
retirement and estate planning. To date, most good financial
planners have been trained as accountants, lawyers, bankers,
insurance agents, or stockbrokers. Some colleges now have
formal programs in financial planning.

Unfortunately, there are as yet no federal or state statutory
educational or professional requirements, testing programs, or
licensing procedures for financial planners, as there are for
attorneys, physicians, real estate brokers, and insurance brokers. That means that anyone can use the title "financial
planner," no matter how little training they may have had.
The result is, in some cases, fraud and abuse. A survey
conducted in 20 states found 22,000 investors had lost $400
million as a result of fraud and abuse in the financial planning industry over a two-year period.

Although about 250,000 people use the title "financial

planner," only about one in five have validated their profes-
sionalism by meeting the requirements for certification by and
becoming a member of one of five professional registries.
Those include:

▶ Organization: Institute of Certified Financial Planners
2 Denver Highlands
10065 East Harvard Avenue
Denver, CO 80231
(800) 282-7526
(303) 751-7600
Designation: C.F.P. (Certified Financial Planner)
Requirements: Certified Financial Planners must:

- Complete a two-year, six-part program conducted
  by the College for Financial Planning. The six
  parts are:

  Introduction to Financial Planning
  Risk Management
  Investments
  Tax Planning and Management
  Retirement Planning and Employee Benefits
  Estate Planning

- Pass extensive tests
- Meet ethical standards set and enforced by the International Board of Standards and Practices for Certified Financial Planners
- Take at least 30 hours of continuing education instructions each year to keep up to date

Publications: *First Steps to Financial Security: A Guide
for Selecting a Certified Financial Planner*
Financial Planning: Past, Present, and Future
Both publications are free.
Referral services: Will provide free list of Certified Finan-
cial Planners in your area

▶ Organization: American College
                 270 Bryn Mawr Avenue
                 Bryn Mawr, PA 19010
                 (215) 526-1000
Designation: Ch.F.C. (Chartered Financial Consultant)
Requirements: To obtain the designation, individuals
   must:
   • Have three years' experience as a planner
   • Pass 10 two-hour examinations
Referral service: Will provide free list of Chartered
   Financial Consultants in your area

▶ Organization: International Association for Financial
                 Planning
                 2 Concourse Parkway
                 Atlanta, GA 30328
                 (800) 241-2148
Designation: R.F.P.P. (Registry of Financial Planning
   Practitioners)
Requirements: To obtain the designation, individuals
   must:
   • Have financial planning as their major vocation
   • Meet a degree related to planning
   • Have at least three years' experience
   • Submit references from five clients
   • Pass a four-hour written exam
   • Participate in continuing education
Referral: Publishes a Directory of Registry Financial
   Planners ($2.50). Will provide free referral to
   practitioners in your area
Note: This association has 24,000 members, but only
   1,000 have earned the designation R.F.P.P.

▶ Organization: International Association of Registered
                 Financial Planners
                 4127 West Cypress Street
                 Tampa, FL 33607
                 (813) 875-7352

Designation: R.F.P. (Registered Financial Planner)
Requirements: To earn the designation, individuals
  must:
  • Have a college degree in economics, business, law,
    or another subject related to financial planning
  • Pass either a state exam to become an insurance
    agent or the National Association of Securities
    curities exam
  • Have four years' experience
  • Participate in continuing education programs
Referral: Will send names of three R.F.P.s in your area
  upon receipt of a self-addressed stamped envelope

▶ Organization: National Association of Personal
                 Financial Advisors
                 1130 Lake Cook Road, Suite 105
                 Buffalo Grove, IL 60089
                 (708) 537-7722
Designation: None
Requirements: Members must:
  • Have education related to financial planning
  • Meet continuing education requirements
  • Charge clients fees only, not commissions
Publications: Brochure explaining fee-only planning and
  a disclosure form to fill out for a prospective planner
  (free)
Referral: Will provide free list of names, educational
  backgrounds, and years of experience for members
  in your area

In addition to referrals from the above organizations, you
should also ask for referrals from your lawyer, accountant,
credit counselor, or friends with similar financial situations.
When you review the backgrounds of all the referrals, you
may find that they present one or more of the following
additional credentials:

- *C.F.A. (Chartered Financial Analyst)* signifies that the person has passed three very rigorous examinations covering a broad range of investment topics. Successful candidates spend an average of 450 hours studying for the exam, and they must meet rigid ethical standards.
- *C.L.U. (Chartered Life Underwriter)* signifies that the person has completed course work, passed examinations, and acquired the experience necessary to earn this designation as a highly qualified insurance agent. This designation is granted by American College, which also designates the Ch.F.C.
- *M.S.F.S. (Master of Sciences in Financial Services)* signifies considerable course work at the American College over and above that necessary to earn the Ch.F.C.
- *J.D. (Juris Doctor)* signifies an attorney who has completed a minimum of three years of law school and has passed the bar examination to practice in that state.
- *C.P.A. (Certified Public Accountant)* signifies a highly trained accountant who has passed very rigorous examinations.
- *Registered Investment Advisor* signifies any person who provides advice on the purchase of specific securities, and who is registered with the Securities and Exchange Commission. Such registration filters out individuals with criminal records or past violations of securities regulations, but it doesn't indicate any experience or skill.
- *Reg. Rep. (Registered Representative)* signifies that the individual has passed extensive examinations that allow him or her to act as a broker of securities.

For more information about selecting a financial planner:

▶ Pamphlet: *What You Should Know About Financial Planners*
  Cost: Free
  From: New York State Department of Law
        Office of Public Information
        120 Broadway
        New York, NY 10271

▶ Booklet: *How to Talk to and Select: Financial Planners,
   Lawyers, Tax Preparers, Real Estate Brokers*
   Cost: Free
   From: AARP
         1909 K Street NW
         Washington, DC 20049

▶ Study: *Financial Planning Abuse: A Growing Problem*
   Cost: Free
   From: Consumer Federation of America
         1424 16th Street NW
         Washington, DC 20036

10

How to Protect Your Pension Rights and Benefits

As we saw in Part I of this book, Social Security laws provide significant protections for recipients as well as a formal appeals system that gives everyone several opportunities to correct mistakes and overturn unfavorable decisions. In addition, constituent pressure leads members of Congress to act as vigorous watchdogs who attempt to ensure that the system operates fairly.

Unfortunately, the 76 million Americans participating in private pension programs do not enjoy such significant protection. As we have seen, the federal government regulates only certain aspects of pension plans, and the Department of Labor has a very limited staff to uncover violations of these laws. The result, as Senate Republican Leader Robert Dole recently pointed out, is that every individual must assume responsibility for defending his or her pension rights. This involves:

- Understanding federal regulation of the pension system
- Understanding the federal pension guarantee system
- Taking advantage of your right to appeal pension decisions
- Monitoring the administration of your pension fund
- Safeguarding your vested pension rights when you leave a job
- Taking action to defend your rights

UNDERSTANDING FEDERAL REGULATION OF THE PENSION SYSTEM

First, it is important to understand what federal pension laws do not do. They do not:

- Require any employer to offer a pension plan
- Guarantee you a pension unless you have satisfied plan requirements
- Specify monetary amounts of pension benefits
- Protect the following benefits often included in a company's retirement package:

> Severance pay
> Vacation pay
> Bonuses and profit sharing
> Medical insurance or benefits
> Disability or accident insurance
> Life insurance
> Stock options or purchase plans
> Prepaid legal service plans

Federal regulations also apply only to pension plans of employers who are engaged in business or in any activity affecting business. They do not cover pension plans offered by:

- Governments
- Religious groups
- Plans with a majority of recipients outside the United States

The Federal Employment Retirement Security Act, amended by the Retirement Equity Act of 1984 and the Tax Reform Act of 1986, sets forth regulations in four general areas to:

1. Prevent discrimination on the basis of sex, race, age, religion, or occupation in determining who can participate in or benefit from a plan
2. Set forth minimum standards for pension plan eligibility, vesting, and payment of survivor benefits

3. Require specific information about the pension plan be made available to participants
4. Ensure that pension funds are invested prudently and honestly

We discuss some of these federal regulations in preceding chapters. If you have any questions about whether your plan is complying with federal law, you should contact:

▶ Organization: Division of Technical Assistance and
                Inquiries
                Pension and Welfare Benefits
                Administration
                U.S. Department of Labor
                200 Constitution Avenue NW
                Washington, DC 20210
                (202) 523-8776

UNDERSTANDING THE FEDERAL PENSION GUARANTEE SYSTEM

In 1974, Congress established the Pension Benefit Guaranty Corporation (PBGC) to administer a program that guarantees payment of basic retirement benefits to participants in most defined benefit pension plans. The PBGC does not guarantee defined contribution programs, because these pension plans do guarantee specific benefits. The federal guarantee fund is financed by contributions from covered pension plans or the employers who sponsor these plans.

The primary function of the PBGC is to protect pension plan participants when a plan is terminated. There are two basic kinds of termination:

1. *A standard termination* results when an employer ends a program for business reasons, often because of mergers or acquisitions. In order to terminate a plan under such circumstances, the plan administrator must prove to the

PBGC that the fund has sufficient assets to guarantee all pension benefits payable to participants in the plan. When such proof is provided, the PBGC allows the employer to purchase an annuity from an insurance company that guarantees that all the plan's legal obligations now and in the future will be met.

2. *A distress termination* results when a plan does not have enough money to meet its obligations, most frequently because of bankruptcy. In this case, the PBGC determines if the plan has enough money to provide the basic benefits guaranteed under federal law. If the plan does not have enough money, the PBGC takes over administration of the plan as trustee and supplements whatever assets the plan has with additional money from the insurance fund.

In distress termination, the PBGC guarantees only *basic benefits*, which are primarily the monthly benefit payable at normal retirement age, the survivor benefit payable at normal retirement age, and some early retirement benefits. The PBGC does not guarantee health and welfare benefits, vacation pay, or other elements of a retirement package.

Federal law places a cap on the monthly benefit that is guaranteed. For pension plans ending in 1990, the maximum monthly payment guaranteed was $1,909.09. Participants whose plans are terminated in distress lose any benefits above this level.

If you participate in a defined benefits plan, your summary plan description should state that your benefits are insured. If you have any questions about whether or not your benefits are insured or what part of your benefits are guaranteed, you can contact the PBGC at:

▶ Organization: Pension Benefit Guaranty Corporation
Coverage and Inquiries Branch
2020 K Street NW
Washington, DC 20006
(202) 778-8800

TAKING ADVANTAGE OF YOUR RIGHT TO APPEAL PENSION DECISIONS

Federal law requires that your employer establish a formal appeals process that you could turn to if:

• You are unfairly denied credit for years of service.
• You disagree with the percentage of benefits that are vested.
• Your claim for benefits was denied.
• You feel your monthly benefit was computed improperly.

Your plan administrator must provide information about this appeals process. Your employer is also prohibited from taking any punitive action against you because you appeal a decision involving your pension plan.

If the decision goes against you, you have the right to pursue civil legal action against your employer. If your pension plan does not have an appeals process, if your request for an appeal is denied, or if you feel you were discriminated against because you appealed, you should immediately contact:

▶ Organization: Division of Technical Assistance and
  Inquiries
  Pension and Welfare Benefits
  Administration
  U.S. Department of Labor
  200 Constitution Avenue NW
  Washington, DC 20210
  (202) 523-8776

MONITORING THE ADMINISTRATION OF YOUR PENSION FUND

Federal law requires that pension funds be invested prudently. One important provision in the *prudence rule* limits a pension fund's investment in company securities to no more than 10 percent of the fund's assets. The law also prohibits mingling pension funds with other corporate funds or loaning significant portions of the fund to the corporation.

Each year your employer must file an annual report for your pension that includes:

- Financial statements showing the current values of your plan's assets and liabilities
- Receipts and disbursements
- Employer contributions
- Schedules of assets held for investment purposes
- Uncollectible or defaulted loans and leases
- Detailed information on transactions in the employer's stock and on transactions that exceed 3 percent of the plan's assets
- Insurance data
- An opinion of an independent qualified public accountant
- Actuarial information and the opinion of an actuary

It's difficult for someone without accounting or financial training to gauge the true financial health of a pension plan from an annual report. However, you can pick up some clues by looking for the following information:

- How much did the plan's assets increase in value over the last year? The last five years? The last 10 years? Every fund will have bad investment years, especially those in which the stock market fell dramatically. But a well-managed fund should show at least an 8 percent to 10 percent annual growth rate over the last decade.
- How much did the employer contribute to the fund last year? If contributions fell dramatically, it either means that the pension plan is overfunded or that the employer has financial problems.
- What kind of assets does the fund hold for investment? A fund that has invested heavily in real estate and commercial loans may face large losses through defaults.
- How much money did the fund lose through uncollectible or

defaulted loans and leases? If this figure is high, the fund's managers have not been investing wisely.

If you suspect that your pension fund might be in financial trouble, you should contact someone with expertise who can go over the annual report with you: your attorney, banker, financial planner, stockbroker, or a knowledgeable friend. Then you can decide whether or not to pursue some of the actions to defend your rights that we discuss later in this chapter.

SAFEGUARDING YOUR PENSION RIGHTS WHEN YOU LEAVE YOUR JOB

Federal law requires that your plan administrator provide the following information when you leave your job:

- A statement of your total accrued pension benefits and the percentage that is vested
- A statement of the nature, amount, and form of deferred vested pension benefits to which you are entitled

If you are entitled to vested benefits under a defined benefit plan, it may be decades before you file a claim. If you disagree with the statements you receive or don't understand the benefits to which you are entitled, you should make an appointment with the plan administrator to solve the problems before you leave the company.

You must also inform the company immediately every time you move. If the plan administrator does not know where to reach you, you may lose benefits if the plan is changed or terminated. You should also contact the plan administrator several months before you plan to retire to obtain information about filing a claim for your vested benefits.

If you have participated in a defined contribution program, you may receive some or all of the funds in your pension account as a lump sum when you leave your job. You must *roll over* these funds into an Individual Retirement Account, your pension account administered by your new employer, or another acceptable pension fund. If you don't, you will have to pay taxes and penalties on the entire amount. If the lump sum is large, you might benefit from the assistance of a financial planner (see Chapter 9).

TAKING ACTION TO DEFEND YOUR RIGHTS

As was pointed out before, the increase in corporate bankruptcies, mergers, and acquisitions has led to an increase in pension problems for many plan participants. In attempting to safeguard your pension rights and monitor your pension plan, you many find that:

- Your plan administrator fails to supply you with plan documents you are entitled to under federal law
- Your appeal concerning your rights or benefits has been unfairly denied
- You are unable to secure your right to future benefits
- You feel that your pension fund has been managed imprudently or invested illegally

In these situations, you have the right to request an investigation of your pension fund by the Secretary of Labor and to file a civil law suit against your employer. You should submit your request along with all available documents and information to:

▶ Organization: Division of Technical Assistance and
Inquiries
Pension and Welfare Benefits
Administration
U.S. Department of Labor
200 Constitution Avenue NW
Washington, DC 20210

You should also send a copy of all materials submitted to the Department of Labor to your Congressman. Your Congressman may be able to influence the Department's decision to take action, particularly if the issues you raise affect a large number of the participants in your plan.

Federal law allows the Secretary of Labor to take civil action if the employer has breached any financial duty or obligation, engaged in any illegal financial transactions, or has refused to provide plan documents or information. Federal law prohibits the Secretary, however, from legal action to resolve disputes about the benefits or rights of any single employee or group of employees.

If the Department of Labor has not acted on your complaint within a reasonable length of time, or if the Department informs you that it will not take action, you have the right to file a civil suit in a local federal district court. A 1990 Congressional study found that such lawsuits were the most successful current method of preventing pension plan abuse and fraud.

Of course, legal action can result in considerable expense. However, you may be able to obtain free or low-cost legal assistance from the resources listed in Chapter 5. You can also get advice on obtaining legal assistance from:

▶ Organization: The Pension Rights Center
918 16th Street NW, Suite 704
Washington, DC 20006

$$=== 11 ===$$

How to Protect Your Pension Rights and Benefits as a Widow or Divorced Spouse

A recent study by the Older Women's League and a hearing held by the House Subcommittee on Retirement Income and Employment both came to the same conclusion: Older women's income has been falling further and further behind older men's income over the last two decades. Among the statistics from the study by the Older Women's League:

- The median income for men age 65 and older was $11,854; the median income for women age 65 and older was $6,734.
- 72 percent of the elderly poor were women.
- Half the widows with incomes below the poverty line were not poor before their husbands' deaths.
- Women's pension income was 73 percent of men's pension income in 1974, but only 54 percent of men's income in 1987.
- Only 25 percent of women receive private or public pensions.
- Only 3 percent of women receive any kind of surviving spouse pension benefits.

In 1984, Congress passed legislation requiring pension plans to provide a joint survivor benefit to all eligible retirees. However, this benefit can legally be as low as 50 percent of the regular retirement benefit payable to the worker alone, and it is payable only to a retiree and his or her spouse at the time of retirement. While pressure mounts on Congress to enact further laws to correct inequities involving surviving spouses, you can take the following steps to protect your retirement income should you be divorced or widowed.

MAINTAIN AN UP-TO-DATE ESTATE FILE

Many Americans don't bother to organize their important financial records and documents. As a result, their surviving spouses and families may be unaware of major assets, including bank accounts, insurance policies, and vested pension benefits from current or former employers. For your protection, you and your spouse should create an estate file that includes:

- Names, addresses, and telephone numbers of accountants, tax preparers, lawyers, financial planners, stockbrokers, and other people important to an estate
- A list of all savings and investments, including bank accounts, stocks, bonds, mutual funds, investment real estate, with account numbers and approximate value
- Tax returns and tax documents from all previous years
- Copies of the summary plan descriptions, survivor coverage data, personal benefits statements, and all other pension-related documents
- A list of all debt, with names and addresses of creditors with account numbers
- A list of all important papers, such as income tax returns, birth and marriage certificates, military discharge papers, automobile and home titles, with location of the papers
- Complete information about safe-deposit boxes, with inventories of the contents of each box

A valuable workbook that will make this task easier is:

▶ Workbook: *Your Vital Papers Logbook*
   Cost: $6.95 ($4.35 AARP members) plus $1.75 postage
   From: AARP Books/Scott, Foresman and Co.
         1865 Miner Street
         Des Plaines, IL 60016

MAKE SURE YOUR SPOUSE HAS ELECTED TO RECEIVE A JOINT SURVIVOR BENEFIT

As of 1985, federal law mandated that a worker could not waive the right to receive a joint survivor benefit without the signature of the spouse. However, that requirement is sometimes ignored. Some workers anxious to receive the highest immediate pension payment put pressure on a spouse to waive the right to a lower joint benefit or even forge a spouse's signature.

If you find out after the death of your spouse that your rights to survivor benefits had been illegally waived, you can defend your right to receive payments by following the advice in Chapter 10.

CONTRIBUTE TO AN INDIVIDUAL RETIREMENT ACCOUNT OR MAINTAIN A LIFE INSURANCE POLICY

Even if you don't work, you and your spouse can contribute up to $2,250 per year to an Individual Retirement Account, and up to $2,000 of that amount can be in your name. Even modest contributions over the years that accrue tax-free interest can provide retirement income that prevents financial hardship.

A second valuable asset can be a life insurance policy.

Many workers drop life insurance coverage when their children are grown. However, life insurance policies that have cash values can be kept in effect until retirement at virtually no cost to the policyholder after the first few years. If your spouse's pension plan has poor survivor benefits, you should explore the purchase of life insurance with a reputable agent.

DEFEND YOUR RIGHTS TO ALIMONY AND CHILD SUPPORT IF YOU ARE DIVORCED

Many divorced women who are entitled to court-ordered alimony or child support payments give up attempting to collect from their ex-husbands. Others assume that they are unable to collect when their ex-spouses retire because they have heard that Social Security and pension benefits cannot be legally *attached* or garnished (that is, seized to pay a legal judgment).

However, court-ordered domestic support payments are the only legal obligations for which both Social Security and pension benefits can be attached. In fact, it is often easier for an ex-spouse to attach such benefits than to track down an ex-spouse who may change jobs or residences frequently before retirement. If you believe your ex-spouse is retired and you are owed monthly support payments, contact one of the legal assistance resources listed in Chapter 5.

EDUCATE YOURSELF ABOUT YOUR RIGHTS AS A SURVIVING OR DIVORCED SPOUSE

Every spouse who fears financial troubles in the retirement years should send for the following information:

▶ Booklet: *Protect Yourself: A Woman's Guide to Pension Rights*
Cost: Free

From: AARP
       1909 K Street NW
       Washington, DC 20049

▶ Booklet: *Facts About the Joint and Survivor Benefits
  for the Retirement Equity Act*
  Cost: Free
  From: Office of Public Affairs
         Pension and Welfare Benefits Administration
         U.S. Department of Labor
         200 Constitution Avenue NW
         Washington, DC 20210

▶ Book: *Changing the Pension Odds for Displaced
  Homemakers*
  Cost: $5.00
  From: Displaced Homemakers Network
         1010 Vermont Avenue NW
         Washington, DC 20005

▶ Booklet: *Older Women and Pensions*
  Cost: $3.50
  From: Older Women's League
         1325 G Street NW
         Washington, DC 20005

INDEX